Industrial Wagons

Compiled by
David Monk-Steel

**INDUSTRIAL RAILWAY SOCIETY
2005**

Published by the **INDUSTRIAL RAILWAY SOCIETY**
at 24, Dulverton Road, Melton Mowbray, Leicestershire, LE13 0SF

www.irsociety.co.uk

ISBN 1 901556 33 6

© Industrial Railway Society 2005

COVER PHOTOGRAPHS
Front cover: One of a large fleet of standard gauge side tipper wagons used for spoil disposal at Wheldale Colliery, Castleford, West Yorkshire, 9/12/1981 (Adrian Booth)

Rear cover: A train of slab ingots (still in their moulds) being worked from the BOS Plant casting bay at British Steel's Scunthorpe Works in the complex of buildings just visible behind the train to the Plate Mill off to the left. For easier handling and safety considerations the train is 'topped and tailed' by Hunslet Bo-Bo locomotives, with 72 (Hunslet 7283 of 1972) nearest the camera. Note also the use of reach wagons to prevent over-exposure of the locomotives' radiators to intense heat from the hot ingots (David Monk-Steel)

Design and production by Harborne Data Services. www.harbornedata.co.uk
Printed by Counter Print, 17 Browning Street, Stafford, ST16 3AX

CONTENTS

INDUSTRIAL WAGONS : AN INTRODUCTION

What is an industrial wagon?

I have defined industrial internal user wagons as privately owned railway wagons that are hauled exclusively by industrial locomotives, or operate over non locomotive worked lines.

Many of these vehicles may have previously been registered or owned by a mainline railway company for general use over the national railway network, but in most cases the registration will have lapsed, and the vehicles are no longer permitted over the public network, although in exceptional circumstances a few privately owned internal wagons were permitted to work for very short distances (usually less than 7 miles) over the main line company tracks without registration, and thus I have taken the liberty to include them in this study.

There were some particular examples of this type of working, such as that in the Sheffield area where industrial wagons were permitted to cross the BR Eastern Region's line at Ickles near Rotherham, hauled by steelworks locomotives, from Holmes Stockyard to the Templeborough Works of Steel, Peech & Tozer loaded with scrap metal. These wagons were subject to much unintentional physical abuse because of the nature of their duties, so to safeguard the main line, a steel company employee was instructed to walk the route after every movement and confirm by telephone that all the wagons and their load had arrived into the sidings at Templeborough and nothing had been left on the track. The signalman was also able to witness most of the movement as it started from behind Ickles signal box and continued in clear view when on BR property.

A spectacular internal wagon movement occurred just north of Sheffield. This involved multi-axle flatbed wagons loaded with large steel forging ingots up to 300 ton gross individual loaded weight travelling across BR lines between the British Steel (former English Steel Corporation) Grimesthorpe and River Don Works. The wagons used in these movements still qualify within my definition because despite being hauled by BR locomotives they did not require main-line registration.

A number of colliery systems in the north-east of England had running powers over NER/LNER metals for many years. In particular, the Lambton, Hetton & Joicey Collieries Ltd (later National Coal Board) had such trains running between Penshaw and Sunderland into BR days. In NCB days a regime of inspection and authorisation existed where each wagon carried a painted coupling symbol showing an examination date indicating that it met the constructional requirements necessary for this operation.

This book is an introductory survey of the neglected subject of internal users, concentrating on the final years of the 20th century. There is good reason for this since before about 1975 the study of railway wagons in any way was very much a minority interest, and except for those enthusiasts engaged in railway modelling, what was found behind the engine buffers was hardly noticed. There are now some good books on the wagon stock of the 'Big Four' railways, main line Private Owners and British Railways, but standard gauge internal user privately owned wagons are ignored almost entirely.

This is the world of incredibly big and very small, ranging from the huge multi-axle 350 tonne iron torpedo ladles that run between Redcar and Lackenby on Teesside, to the little ammunition van from the RNAD at Bedenham, Hampshire, little more than a shed on wheels.

Most industrial wagons, principally because of the nature of their duties and loads, are mundane and scruffy. The general service wagons employed in steelworks are typical, being constructed and repaired locally using steel plate and section that came most readily to hand, and rarely if ever receiving a coat of paint, save for the fleet number crudely painted at one end and the tare weight at the other. These humble vehicles were usually constructed on the chassis of old mainline wagons that had served their time, and when they were beyond economic repair were unceremoniously added to the scrap pile, with their final rail journey inside one of their cousins to the melting shop.

Collieries, too, operated large numbers of coal wagons too old to venture on to the main line, and examples of these are discussed in the main text.

Purpose-built internal user wagons are of particular interest because they usually have special tasks to perform. The steel industry needed a considerable variety of such wagons and the duties they were required to perform usually involved hot and/or heavy loads. Several types are included in this book, but by their very nature (and immediate environment) it was not easy or safe to get close to them for in-detail study, and the steelworks managers were quite understandably reluctant to allow visits to observe, photograph and measure such equipment. It was therefore a rare privilege to be able to get near some of these items, usually during annual works shut down, or in one or two melancholy cases shortly after the works itself had ceased to operate forever.

I have confined my study to standard gauge wagons because I have acquired a great deal more information about them and also consider that narrow gauge wagons are covered in other publications in far greater detail than I could provide, and by people far more knowledgeable about them.

A few wagons illustrated have been measured in detail, or the dimensions are recorded against the original diagram issued by British Railways prior to being sold out of service. Unfortunately, not all wagons have been measured, but wherever possible an estimate has been made and the basic dimensions are included.

Many of the wagons covered by this book no longer exist and they did not always carry builder's plates or other distinguishing marks to indicate their origins. Their industrial owners, when questioned about their origins, simply stated that they had been purchased from another concern, or that records were not available. Records may come to light in the future, but until they do a lot of the data recorded here is based upon a reasonable amount of detective work and even more guesswork. For this I can do no more than apologise. Finally, a plea that if you have information which may correct or enhance that given in this publication please do not keep it yourself but share it with other members of the Industrial Railway Society. I will be happy to facilitate this.

I hope readers derive as much pleasure from this book as I did in compiling it. All pictures were taken by the author in the year shown, unless otherwise credited.

Acknowledgements

None of this would have been possible without the assistance of representatives of industry, the Ministry of Defence, British Railways, preservation sites and dozens of fellow enthusiasts, both inside and outside the IRS. I would like to put on record my thanks to the managers and staff of Allied Steel & Wire, Cardiff; Associated Portland Cement Manufacturers at Swanscombe and Greenhithe; British Rail at Tinsley, Worksop, Tyne Yard, Tees Yard, and York; British Steel (and its successors) at Aldwarke and Ickles (both Rotherham), Lackenby, Orgreave, Ravenscraig, Scunthorpe, Stocksbridge, and Workington; Ford's at Dagenham; ICI Tunstead; Ministry of Defence, Army Department, at Bishopton, Marchwood and Long Marston; the National Coal Board in Northumberland, Durham and South Yorkshire; National Smokeless Fuels in Derbyshire; Seaham Harbour; Tyne and Wear Metro; the Bowes Railway at Springwell; the Rutland Railway Museum at Cottesmore; the Stephenson Museum at Percy Main; and the Tanfield Railway at Marley Hill. Also the following individuals: Paul Bartlett, Brian Cuttell, Dr Peter Holmes, Dr Peter Fidczuk, Paul James, David Larkin, Trevor Lodge, Trevor Mann, Greg Martin, Roger Monk, David Ratcliffe, Mark Saunders, Roger Silsbury, Hywel Thomas, and many more.

David Monk-Steel
15 Chelwood Walk
Holgate
YORK
YO26 4UH

STANDARD GAUGE INDUSTRIAL INTERNAL USER RAILWAY WAGONS OF THE LATER PART OF THE 20th CENTURY

General Notes

Wagons which were used internally on private railway systems came in all shapes and sizes depending upon their intended use, the size and nature of the system and their origin.

The uses to which wagons might be put were as varied as the businesses that operated them. In this book a selection of wagons observed during the last 20 years of the 20th Century are illustrated, in most cases at work. In a book of this size only a sample of the vehicles can be illustrated and every attempt has been made for this to be representative. There is no officially published information about these fleets most of which followed a shadowy existence ignored by officialdom and enthusiast alike. The notes and pictures are the product of activities by enthusiasts, usually aided by company officials, but except in a very few cases the information cannot be backed by validated documentary evidence. Officials would tolerate (usually) requests to take pictures and would speak about current uses, but were generally less keen to grant access to files and records. Quite often records did not exist, and even the surviving wagon builders, when approached, were ignorant of the later history of their products. There is therefore a fair degree of educated guesswork, particularly relating to the early days.

The types of wagon observed and the uses to which they were being put can be summarised into the following categories allied to the industries that they served.

Engineering

An engineering construction plant or a ship yard often operated a modest fleet of flat wagons, basically a frame carried upon four wheels, to carry steel plate and section around the site, to be loaded and unloaded by cranes and to be as versatile as possible.

Coal

A colliery would often use wagons to haul dirt from the washery to the spoil heap, and generally favoured side tipping wagons for this; and also use mineral or hopper wagons to move coal from the screens to stockpile, canal side, or landsale. In West Cumberland, Northumberland and Durham and in parts of Scotland collieries also used wagons to move coal over private mineral railways to seaports for shipment. With the run down of deep mining there are at time of writing (2004) no locations in England or Scotland operating standard gauge wagons, and only two opencast sites in South Wales known to be operating an internal fleet.

Coke

Coke cars are used to receive hot coke from the coke ovens, transfer it to the quenching tower and then dump it into a hopper for removal. These are large and very robust bogie wagons, operated singly by a special locomotive that can control the discharge equipment remotely. Coke works also used mineral and hopper wagons to carry coal to and from blending, tank wagons to move and store liquid by-products, and hopper wagons to remove coke from the cooling area to storage and distribution.

Iron and Steel

Steelworks used a huge variety of specialist vehicles, and are arguably the most interesting in this respect. Hopper and mineral wagons were used to move raw materials such as coal, coke, limestone and scrap from stockpiles to furnaces (and sometimes from docks to stockpiles); slag ladles were used to remove hot liquid slag from the furnaces to the slag bank; and huge transfer cars or torpedo ladles were used to take molten iron from blast furnaces to the steelplant. The nature of steelplant traffic was highly dependent on the steelmaking and casting processes employed, and the plant layout. Often ladles of liquid steel were transported on rail borne carriages from the furnace bay to the casting bay; the steel could then be teemed into ingot moulds carried on casting cars, and finally the casting cars (or other rail vehicles) took the solidified ingots to the rolling mill or ingot stock yard. Roll wagons were sometimes used to take the different shaped heavy rolls from the roll shop to the rolling mill. Supporting all this process activity would be a fleet of wagons to take away scrap, receive and haul pig iron, billets, bars, sections and coils in huge variety. Steelworks wagons are probably the most specialised and a lot of these fleets were purpose built and extremely massively constructed for the arduous conditions encountered. The small number of plants extant and the specialisation within the steel industry has reduced the opportunities to observe these vehicles, but Corus at Scunthorpe operates a large mixed fleet, and the works at Workington, Teesside, Aldwarke, Stocksbridge and Port Talbot also have internal wagons in daily use. Only the Corus plants at Teesside, Port Talbot and Scunthorpe still move molten iron by rail.

Foundries

Allied to steelworks, foundries also needed tough wagons, and for molten metal transfer special ladle cars were used. St. Gobains Pipelines at Stanton by Dale in Nottinghamshire still moves molten metal by rail.

Quarries

Quarrying in its many forms required fleets of wagons fitted to the purpose. The type of wagon was influenced by the type of loading and discharge arrangements. In most recent examples loading would be by mechanical shovel so an open top high-sided wagon was commonplace. At the point of discharge the wagon design was influenced by the need to empty the load, either by tipping the entire wagon (tippler) or tipping the wagon body whilst the wheels remained in contact with the track (tipper or dump car). Some quarries used hopper bottom wagons but this was less common. There are very few quarries now using their own wagons, although a number use private owner wagons registered to operate on the national network. Most internal movements are now almost exclusively carried out using rubber tyred plant. One of the last, Rugby Cement at Barrington used internal tippler wagons until 4/2005.

Quarries specialising in the cutting of building stone in blocks rather than as aggregate used drop sided wagons, or where very large blocks were required to be hauled, massive 'bogies'. Quarries that operated standard gauge railway wagons to haul blocks were not common, but a few were to be found in association with the upkeep of sea or harbour defences, for example at Holyhead and South Shields.

Docks

Docks and harbours, particularly the larger ones, maintained large fleets of wagons to receive ships' cargo, transfer it to storage areas, and to aid distribution. A feature of dock traffic was that wagons were often employed as mobile warehousing, and might remain under load for weeks. Types of wagon depended on the nature of cargo, but tended to be of the same design as those used by main line railway companies and often contained a high proportion of ex-main line wagons sold out of service. End door minerals, flat wagons, timber bolsters, vans and open wagons of standard design were common. The former railway-owned docks (including the big east coast ports of Goole, Hull, Immingham, Grimsby Tees, and Hartlepool) all possessed massive fleets of wagons and were ultimately owned by the British Transport Docks Board, which obtained all its wagons from British Railways, and it was the British Railways stock registry at Derby that kept these wagon fleet records. The Port of London Authority also maintained a huge fleet of rolling stock of a similar nature, but was independent of BR. The docks at Bristol, on Merseyside, and on Tyneside also had significant rail systems with large wagon fleets. All of these fleets had been scrapped by 1980.

Military

The military also operated significant fleets of rolling stock. The ordinary fleet consisted of vehicles not dissimilar to those of the main line companies with a preponderance of vans and open wagons, but the Army also possessed a large fleet of very special wagons for moving armoured fighting vehicles and similar machines. These wagons were of two distinct types, 'Warflats' and 'Warwells', both types were robustly constructed bogie wagons with either a flat or depressed centre deck respectively. Originally these vehicles were registered for use on the network of Britain, and some were also registered with the UIC (Union Internationale des Chemins de Fer) for operations on mainland Europe. As newer types were introduced, particularly as the hand-brake only types were replaced by those with continuous automatic air brakes, the older vehicles were either retained for use in the stores depots or sold for further use. The Army maintains a significant fleet of wagons at the depots it still operates.

Explosives

Factories that manufactured explosives needed wagons to move chemicals, particularly tank wagons for acid, and also covered vans to move safely the finished product. These vehicles were usually constructed in a manner that minimised the likelihood of a spark or leakage. There are no such standard gauge systems still operating.

Nuclear

BNFL operated a fleet of wagons internally for transferring nuclear fuel during the processing at Sellafield. These consisted of stainless steel clad transfer cars, and a fleet of tank wagons for conveyance of acid within the works was also operated. It has not been possible to obtain pictures of these vehicles or to confirm that they are still in use.

Some notes on common types of wagon

The RCH Mineral wagon

Prior to nationalisation there were half a million privately owned coal wagons on the railways of Britain. Collieries had their 'maids of all work' in the shape of the Railway Clearing House standard design wooden coal wagon. Their basic box shape was little altered from 1887, and limited by the size and shape of the colliery screens and the means of unloading at the destination. Because they were 9ft wheelbase and 15ft over headstocks (16ft 6in from 1923), they were short enough to go round tight curves and fit snugly on wagon turntables and end tipper tables. Their 8ft 9in maximum height and 8ft 3in maximum width avoided fouling the colliery screens loading equipment. A high degree of standardisation was necessary because a damaged or defective wagon had to be capable of being repaired anywhere on the national network, and this avoided the shipment of bespoke parts to return a wagon to service, thus saving time.

Prior to 1939 collieries tended to own large fleets of these wagons, and most were registered for running on the main lines. If wagons were needed to move coal to and from stock the collieries could use vehicles taken from these fleets, although they did have the option to use older wagons kept back as internal users when the requirements of registration made them beyond economic repair. The collieries were nationalised in 1947 but the entire fleet of colliery owned private owner wagons had already passed into government control, together with merchants' and wagon hirers' fleets, as a war-time measure in 1940. These 600,000 former privately owned wagons did not return to private ownership but on the formation of British Railways in 1948 were nationalised. These vehicles were in poor structural condition because of difficulties of maintenance, caused by shortages of materials and labour during war-time. Fortunately in 1938 the Railway Clearing House had embarked on a programme to replace the 12 ton wooden wagon with a 14 ton capacity steel one. During the war this design was improved to carry 16 tons, and the Ministry of War Transport Department organised the construction of these as part of the war effort. As soon as steel shortages eased the main line railways started building 16 tonners, and the old wood bodied 12 tonner became obsolete. The flood of steel body wagons released the wooden ones for scrap or sale, and many former private owner wagons were bought back from BR by the NCB for internal use in collieries after the collieries were nationalised in 1947. Prior to that date collieries had used their own fleets, most of which had been registered for main line running, and would have used them internally as appropriate. Wagons for which registration had expired and which may have still some life left were also retained at a lower level of maintenance, but to prevent them 'escaping' on to the main line they were branded 'for internal use' and usually distinguished by a large white St. Andrew's Cross painted on each side. The use of a horizontal white stripe on the side was less common. The old wagons thus returned to the collieries, and also appeared in large numbers on dock estate lines, especially the docks of the British Transport Docks Board.

Tank wagons

Tank wagons were not nationalised as such during the war nor subsequently, and although subjected to the same Railway Clearing House standardisation were not subjected to such a significant replacement programme as the mineral wagon fleet.

During World War 2 the Air Ministry constructed many modern vehicles for aviation fuel, and following cessation of hostilities these vehicles entered the private owner fleets in some number. Demand for petroleum fuel use was on the upsurge after 1950 so the wholesale replacement of wagons still did not happen immediately. It was not until the late 1950s when new 35 ton gross laden weight vacuum braked vehicles started to appear on the national network, and the traditional handbrake only 14 or 20 ton vehicles were then phased out. The older vehicles were not really a lot of use for other purposes as they stood, so the option to sell them on for internal use was on the face of it a non-starter. However, once the tank itself was removed the steel chassis was ideal for rebuilding, either as a flat bogie, or with a new fabricated body.

A very odd conversion did occasionally appear, with the top half of the tank burned off and the bottom half retained in the cradle as an open wagon of limited capacity (and dubious stability). This ugly re-use in internal service has only been reported twice, at ICI at Tunstead and Brown Bayley's/Hadfields in Sheffield. There may well have been others but none so far have been reported.

Returning to more conventional re-use, the chassis once shorn of tank and cradle was an ideal platform for a variety of body. The most common appears to have been the fitting of an all steel box body to create a general service wagon for steel works purposes. The use of heavy steel plate and rolled section riveted or welded into a strong box was ideal for carrying scrap about in the works and would stand up to any amount of rough handling, especially beneath electro-magnet cranes.

Matters within the oil industry changed further in the 1970s when new wagons appeared. Following this increase of tank wagon capacity to 45 tons gross laden weight and the widespread use of air brakes the 35 tonners became obsolete. By coincidence these too became ideal candidates as chassis donors, and started to appear in steelworks, as scrap carriers, coke hoppers and mineral box wagons.

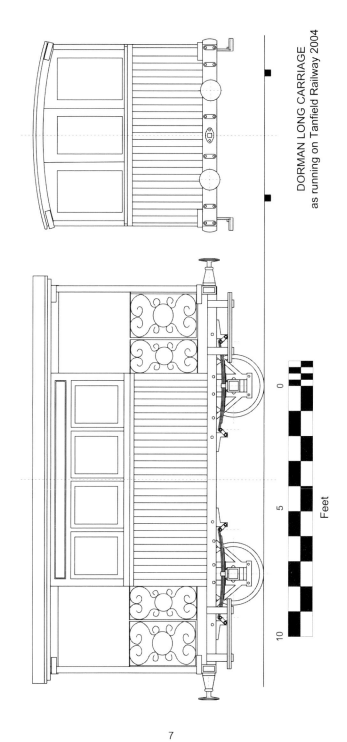

DORMAN LONG CARRIAGE
as running on Tanfield Railway 2004

Feet

0   5   10

INSPECTION CARRIAGE : DORMAN LONG & Co, TEESSIDE

(J. W. Armstrong Trust Collection)

Builder – Darlington Wagon and Engineering Co Ltd

Date Built – 1880

Length – 16ft 5in over headstocks

Wheelbase – 7ft 6in

Height – 9ft 3in

Carrying capacity – 10 persons on bench seats

Location – Dorman Long, Teesside

Purpose – built to carry senior managers and visitors around the Teesside Works of Dorman Long

Livery – probably dark red

Fate – survived to be preserved by the Tanfield Railway in County Durham

Notes – known as the 'Glass Carriage'

BOGIE SECTIONS WAGON : BSC SCUNTHORPE

(Author : October 1994)

Builder - uncertain

Date Built – uncertain

Length – approximately 67 ft

Bogie centres – approximately 48 ft

Height – 5ft 6in approximately rail to deck, 9ft 9in approximately to top of ends

Carrying capacity – 60 tons

Number series – 5601 - 5610

Location – British Steel, Scunthorpe

Purpose – transport of long steel sections within Scunthorpe Steelworks

Livery – unpainted

BOGIE STEEL CARRIER : ALLIED STEEL & WIRE

(Author : August 1999)

Builder – converted by Allied Steel & Wire Ltd, Cardiff, from BR 45 ton slab/coil wagon

Date Built – converted in 1980s

Length – 42ft 0in over headstocks

Bogie Wheelbase – 31ft 6in

Height – 9ft 1½in from rail to top of stanchions

Carrying capacity – originally 45 tons

Number series – BM501 – BM505

Location – Allied Steel & Wire, Cardiff

Purpose – carrying billets within the steelworks

Livery – pale blue bodywork and yellow stanchions

Notes – the vehicle illustrated, BM502, was BR no. B949571 (Swindon 1962, lot 3424). The original wagon had coil cradles over the bogies and in the well, and slab support framing, which have now mostly been removed.

COVERED BULK : BOCM SELBY

(Author : 2003)

Builder – unknown

Date Built – 1940s

Length – 22ft 0ins over headstocks

Wheelbase – 12 ft 0ins

Height – 10ft approximately

Carrying capacity – 20 tons

Location – Selby, North Yorkshire

Purpose – conveys grain from within the mill complex

Livery – blue

Fate – extant and in use January 2004

Notes – it is probable that these vehicles were originally Ministry of Supply 20 ton coal hopper wagons, converted for their present duties by the fitting of an overall roof with loading hatches. These vehicles are unusual in that they have had their spring suspension removed and replaced by wooden blocks, making them rigid frame, although as they are manoeuvred at low speed by a road/rail tractor this is not a significant disadvantage.

BRAKE VAN : NCB ASHINGTON

(Author : 1986)

Builder – British Railways Faverdale, Lot 2741 (B952963)

Date Built – 1955

Length – 24ft 0in over headstocks

Wheelbase – 16ft 0in

Height – 12ft 4¼in over all

Carrying capacity – not applicable (tare 20 tons)

Location – Ashington, Northumberland

Purpose – guard's van on NCB coal trains working over BR lines between Ashington Colliery, Ellington Colliery and Lynemouth

Livery – red with yellow ends

Fate – scrapped or sold; sister vehicles 9300/10 and 9300/12 are preserved at the Rutland Railway Museum, Cottesmore

BRAKE VAN : LAMBTON, HETTON & JOICEY RAILWAY

(Author : 1987)

Builder – Lambton Joicey and Hetton Railway, Philadelphia Works

Date Built – 1946

Length – 16ft 6in approximately

Wheelbase – 11ft 6in

Location – latterly at NCB Seaham Colliery, pictured at Andrews House

Purpose – guards van on coal trains operated by LHJR over LNER metals. Note the heavy end stanchions, extended below normal headstock level to permit buffing up to the dumb buffers of 'Black Wagons', which still could be found in the area, usually on the dock.

Livery – red

Fate – Van No.7 preserved on Tanfield Railway

Notes – built by apprentice Tom Hardy as a craft test

BRAKE VAN : MOD ARMY

(Greg Martin : June 1992)

Builder – Southern Railway, Ashford

Date Built – 1942

Length – 24ft 0in over headstocks

Wheelbase – 16ft 0in

Carrying capacity – not applicable (25t tare)

Number series – ARMY 49001 (registered WS-SR 1015)

Location – Long Marston, 6th June 1992

Purpose – guard's brake van on military trains

Livery – khaki green body, black underframe, yellow lettering

Fate – still extant

Notes – these vans are similar but not identical to SR brakevans. They were built new with vacuum brake whereas the SR vans did not have vacuum brakes.

BOGIE WARFLAT : MOD ARMY

(Greg Martin : June 1993)

Builder – Gloucester C & W Co Ltd

Date Built – 1965

Length – 11.582 metres over headstocks

Wheelbase – 6.858 metres bogie centres

Height – 1.501 metres rail to top of guide rails

Carrying capacity – 54 tons

Location – Marchwood

Purpose – conveying heavy machinery, military and armoured fighting vehicles

Livery – army green with yellow lettering

Fate – extant

Notes – two vehicles numbered 80800 and 80801 are known to have been built. Formerly registered for operation on BR these are now in internal use. This wagon has a temporary cradle for carrying a boat.

BOGIE RAIL CARRIER FLAT – CORUS WORKINGTON

(Author : August 2001)

Builder – Head Wrightson & Co Ltd

Date Built – 1955

Length – 66ft 1in over headstocks

Wheelbase – 46ft 0in

Height – 5ft from rail to top of bolters

Carrying capacity – 50 tons

Location – Corus, Workington

Purpose – formerly BR rail and sleeper wagons, code named 'Sturgeon', (No. 167, the wagon illustrated, was DB994113). These wagons are used in pairs to carry 120 ft rails from the rolling mill to the rail welding plant.

Livery – blue

Fate – still in use in 2004

BAGGED CEMENT FLAT WAGON : APCM SWANSCOMBE

(Author : July 1992)

Builder – APCM Ltd on second hand wagon chassis

Date Built – unknown

Length – variously 17ft 2in. – 18ft 1in

Width – 10ft 0in

Wheelbase – 9ft 0in

Carrying capacity – probably 10 tons

Number series – 13 – 99 (eight vehicles seen in 1994)

Location – Swanscombe

Purpose – conveyed bagged cement from mill to Thames side wharf

Livery – unpainted, coloured white by cement and chalk dust

Height – 3ft 2in from floor to top of end. 4ft rail to floor approximately

Notes – an APCM built flat wagon, constructed on the steel frames of a former chalk tippler wagon. The new floor is 10ft 0in wide to accommodate more bagged cement. The width of the new floor would preclude their use on main line railways, where a ruling maximum body width of about 8ft 0in was common. The wagon is also completely un-braked which would also prohibit its use on the main line. At APCM train movement was arrested by the locomotive brake alone, and secure parking of wagons achieved with wheel chocks or wheel sprags.

The chalk tippers were second hand. Some were originally GER 10 ton open wagons which were eventually rebuilt on new steel underframes at Swanscombe.

CONTAINER FLAT WAGON : FORD DAGENHAM

(Greg Martin : 1988)

Builder – constructed from the underframe of a former BR tube wagon

Date Built – 1959, probably sold and converted during 1970s

Length – 32ft 0in over headstocks

Wheelbase – 18ft 6in

Height – 4ft 0in rail to deck, approximately

Carrying capacity – originally 22 tons

Location – Ford Motor Works, Dagenham, Essex

Purpose – moving containers of car components within Ford Motor Works

Livery – yellow bodywork, buffer beam and buffer shanks with black solebars but with yellow axlebox covers, brake levers and brake lever guide

BOGIE HOPPER WAGON : TYNE & WEAR METRO

(David Ratcliffe : August 1987)

Builder – Ashford, Southern Railway

Date Built – 1947

Length – 32ft 6in over headstocks

Wheelbase – 23ft 0in bogie centres

Height – 9ft 9in from rail

Carrying capacity – 40 tons

Location – North Shields

Purpose – conveying ballast to site of track renewal

Livery – olive green

Fate – scrapped

Notes – four wagons were purchased from BR to assist with track repairs on the Tyne & Wear Metro system

BOGIE BALLAST HOPPER WAGON : LONDON UNDERGROUND

(David Ratcliffe : April 1993)

Builder – W.H. Davis, Shirebrook

Date Built – 1981

Carrying capacity – 30 tons

Number series – HW201 to HW222

Location – used throughout the London Underground system but here seen at West Ruislip

Purpose – delivery of stone ballast to all parts of LUL railway system,

Fate – still in service

Notes – this is a modern London Transport bogie hopper wagon. It is designed to travel through tube tunnels so it has been built to the smaller tunnel gauge, and is fitted with both automatic and hook and link couplings and retractable buffers to enable it to be hauled by battery locomotives or locomotives with normal drawgear.

COAL HOPPER : LAMBTON, HETTON & JOICEY RAILWAY

(Author : 1985)

Builder – LHJR (NCB) Philadelphia Workshops

Date Built – 1940s

Length – 16ft 6in

Wheelbase – 10ft 6in

Height – 8ft 3in approximately

Carrying capacity – 15 tons

Location – NCB Ashington

Purpose – internal transport of coal on the NCB Lambton Railway system

Livery – red with black ironwork

Fate – scrapped or sold

Notes – these vehicles, purpose built for the collieries, followed a traditional design used by the NER. Early versions had lower sides with a capacity of 10½ tons, but they evolved to this larger 15 ton variety seen here, and on the main line a 20 ton version became the standard.

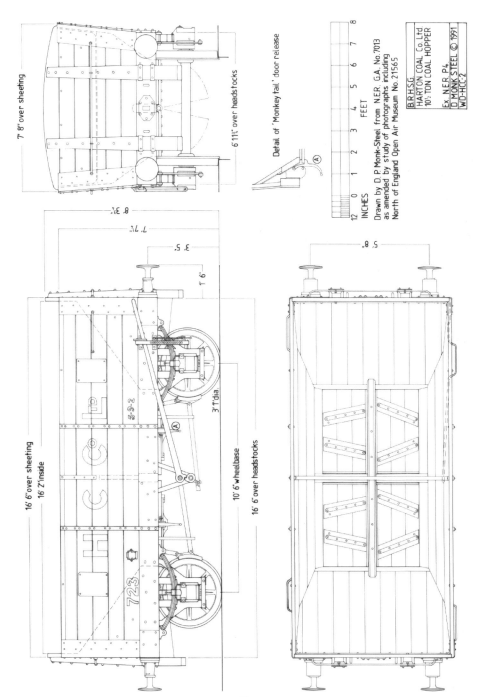

7' 8" over sheeting

6' 11½" over headstocks

Detail of 'Monkey tail' door release

(A)

INCHES

12 0   1   2   3   4   5   6   7   8

FEET

Drawn by D.P. Monk-Steel from N.E.R. G.A. No. 7013
as amended by study of photographs including
North of England Open Air Museum No. 21565

B.R.H.S.G.
HARTON COAL Co. Ltd
10½ TON COAL HOPPER

Ex N.E.R. P4
D. MONK STEEL © 1991
WD-HCC-2

8' 3¾"

7' 7½"

3' 5"

1' 6"

16' 6" over sheeting

16' 2" inside

10' 6" wheelbase

16' 6" over headstocks

3' 1" dia.

(A)

5' 8"

723

COAL HOPPER WAGON : NATIONAL COAL BOARD

(Author : September 1986)

Builder – Standard Railway Wagon Co Ltd of Heywood, Lancashire

Date Built – 1955 - 1957

Length – 18ft 0in over headstocks

Wheelbase – 10ft 6in

Livery – originally red with black ironwork and white lettering. Later all black with white letters (1985-6).

Height – 9ft 6in rail to top of side

Carrying capacity – 19 ton, (a 25 ton version was also built between 1958 and 1963)

Number series – 19 tonners - 9300/6001 to 9300/6199, 25 tonners - 9300/11000 to 9300/11225

Location – Ashington, Northumberland

Purpose – carrying coal and mine spoil from the washery to landsale or spoil tip. Wagons of this type were also hauled by NCB locomotives to convey the Alcan power station at Lynemouth partially over British Railways metals.

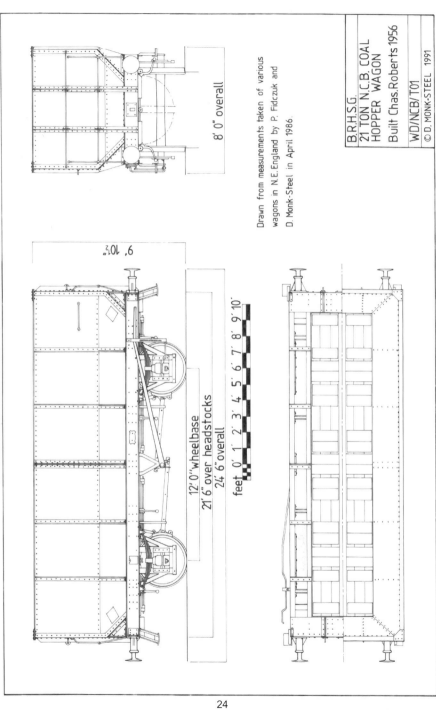

8' 0" overall

Drawn from measurements taken of various wagons in N.E. England by P. Fidczuk and D. Monk-Steel in April 1986.

B.R.H.S.G.
21 TON N.C.B. COAL HOPPER WAGON
Built Chas.Roberts 1956
WD/NCB/T01
© D. MONK-STEEL 1991

9' 10½"

feet 0' 1' 2' 3' 4' 5' 6' 7' 8' 9' 10'

12'0" wheelbase
21' 6" over headstocks
24' 6" overall

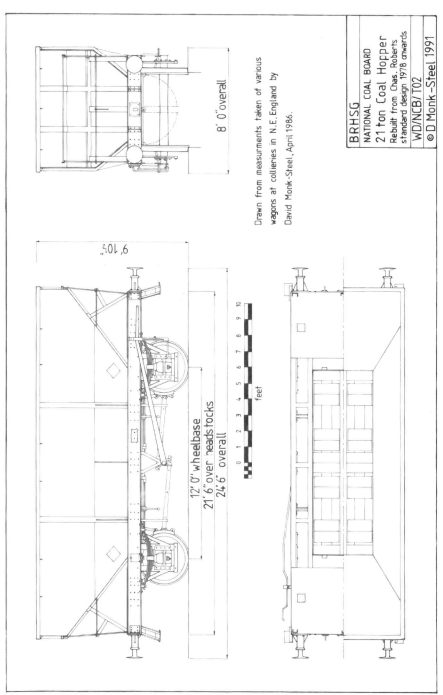

8' 0" overall

9' 10½"

12' 0" wheelbase
21'6" over headstocks
24'6" overall

0 1 2 3 4 5 6 7 8 9 10
feet

Drawn from measurements taken of various
wagons at collieries in N.E. England by
David Monk-Steel, April 1986.

BRHSG
NATIONAL COAL BOARD
21 ton Coal Hopper
Rebuilt from Chas. Roberts
standard design 1978 onwards
WD/NCB/T02
© D. Monk-Steel 1991

25

COAL HOPPER WAGON : NCB DERWENTHAUGH

Date Built – 1956

Height – 9ft 9in

Length – 21ft 6in

Livery – red body, black underframe, white lettering

Purpose – carrying coal from the drift mine discharge point and stockyard to the coke ovens and coke from the quenching area to stockyard, quay or landsale

Fate – scrapped 1985

Wheelbase – 12 ft

Carrying capacity – 20 tons

Builder – Charles Roberts (some also built by Hurst Nelson)

Number series – 6176 – 6237, 6343 – 6937

Location – Derwenthaugh, County Durham. Wagons of this type were found throughout the Durham NCB area.

Notes – wagon 6583 is seen here in almost original condition, most of its contemporaries having been rebodied during the 1970s. Coal was discharged through eight wooden trap doors which were locked and released using 'monkey tail' levers.

COAL HOPPER WAGON : NCB SOUTH HETTON

(Author : 1987)

Builder – Hurst Nelson & Co Ltd, rebuilt by NCB Seaham Wagon Shops

Date Built – 1957, (rebuilt 1978)

Length – 21ft 6in

Wheelbase – 12ft 0in

Height – 9ft 8in

Carrying capacity – 21 tons

Location – NCB South Hetton / Hawthorn Mine

Purpose – conveying mine stone from colliery washer to spoil tip, sea coal to staithes and landsale coal to stock yard

Livery – red with black solebars etc. and white lettering

Number Series – they were numbered in a series starting at 1 and continuing until about 955. It is not certain if there were gaps in this sequence.

Fate – scrapped 1985

Notes – these wagons were similar to the Derwenthaugh riveted 20t hopper wagon when delivered, but were rebuilt with redesigned welded all steel bodies and a reduced number of bottom doors to improve the speed and force of discharge

'BLACK WAGGON' : LONDONDERRY RAILWAY

(Author : August 1986)

Wheelbase – 5ft 0in

Height – 6ft 9in

Length – 12ft 9in over buffers

Built – Lambton, Hetton & Joicey Workshops, Philadelphia, Co.Durham

Restored by – NCB Workshops, Philadelphia, Co. Durham

Location – Seaham Harbour

The 'Black Waggon' (so named after the almost universal livery of black) was a very common type in North East England, it originated from the very earliest days of railways when horse haulage and gravity were the principal means of traction and despite larger wagons appearing with the introduction of mechanical traction the 'Black Waggon' remained in use almost to the end of coal production in Durham and Northumberland.

The simple bearings and primitive brake gear restricted their use latterly to work under the coal staithes at Seaham. This example was a 'gate guardian' at Seaham Harbour, and a few have been saved by local preservation railways.

The low level 'dumb' buffers required locomotives, brake vans and many of the later wagons to be equipped with lower level buffing gear to facilitate interworking.

COAL HOPPER WAGON : NATIONAL SMOKELESS FUELS

(Author : 1987)

Builder – not known

Date Built – not known, but pre-1939

Length – 21ft 6in over headstocks

Wheelbase – 12ft 0in

Height – about 10ft 0in

Carrying capacity – 20 tons

Location – National Smokeless Fuels Ltd. Avenue Coking plant, Wingerworth, Derbyshire

Purpose – transport of coal slack and coke within the coke works

Fate – scrapped when plant closed about 1990.

Notes – these 20 ton coal hopper wagons were formerly privately owned vehicles formerly belonging to Liverpool Corporation Electricity Department and registered to operate over the national network, but were used in more recent years to carry coal within the plant. It is possible that they were requisitioned by the Government in World War 2 and subsequently taken over by BR at nationalisation and sold to National Smokeless Fuels when surplus to requirements. In coke works service they were probably painted black but had become very rusty when seen and no longer carried any form of identification. The large wheel on the side was used to open and close the hopper discharge doors situated between the wheels.

SIDE ELEVATION

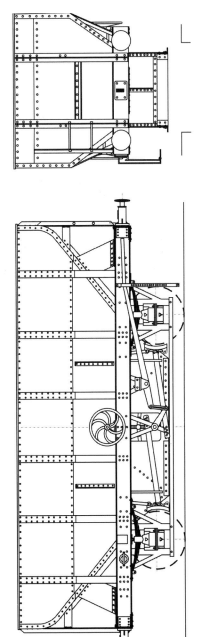

Drawn by D. Monk-Steel from
measurements of BR334 at
Brodsworth, South Yorkshire, taken
by D. Monk-Steel, G. Martin and T.
Mann, , 6th June 1987

0

5

Feet

10

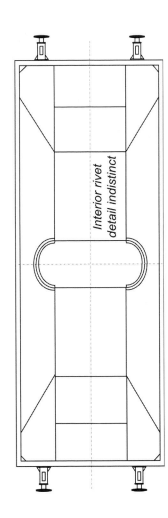

*Interior rivet
detail indistinct*

30

COKE HOPPER WAGON : BSC SCUNTHORPE

(Author : September 1988)

Builder – originally as a tank wagon by Charles Roberts & Co Ltd of Horbury, but rebuilt as a hopper wagon by BSC

Date Built – 1960, converted in 1970s

Length – 23ft 8in approximately

Wheelbase – 15ft 0in

Height – 10ft 0in

Carrying capacity – 20 tons

Location – Scunthorpe

Purpose – carriage of coke from stock to the blast furnaces

Livery – red with white lettering, weathered to black

Fate – scrapped or sold

Notes – built on chassis of a 1960s private owner class 'B' tank wagon

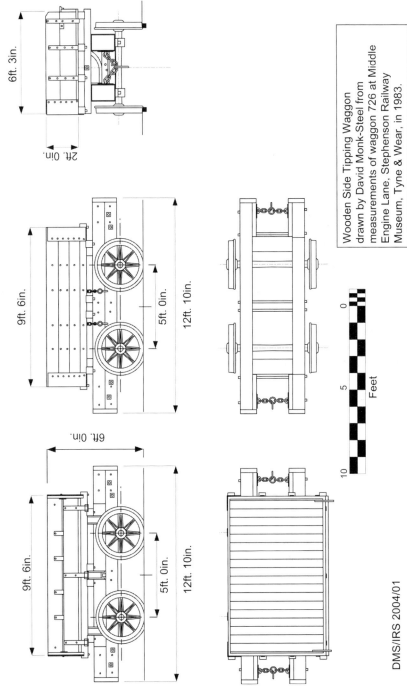

Wooden Side Tipping Waggon drawn by David Monk-Steel from measurements of waggon 726 at Middle Engine Lane, Stephenson Railway Museum, Tyne & Wear, in 1983.

6ft. 3in.

2ft. 0in.

9ft. 6in.

5ft. 0in.

12ft. 10in.

6ft. 0in.

9ft. 6in.

5ft. 0in.

12ft. 10in.

0

5

10

Feet

DMS/IRS 2004/01

32

CONTRACTORS SIDE TIPPING WAGON : STEPHENSON RAILWAY MUSEUM

(Author : 1985)

Date built – not known

Length – 12ft 10in over baulks

Length over body – 9ft 6in

Carrying capacity – 6 tons approximately

Width – 6ft 3in over body

Height – 6ft 0in from rail

Fate – preserved at Middle Engine Lane, seen in 1985, but subsequent fate not known

Notes – this wagon is known generally as a 'Manchester Ship Canal' wagon. The type was widely used by contractors building railways, canals and dams to remove soil and rock, and could be tipped on one side only. Some quarry companies also employed them for removal of overburden, and sometimes for haulage of product. They would often be hauled over rough track by horses.

The wagon pictured here is unidentified, and is in an advanced stage of deterioration; the drop side that should be on this side had fallen off, and the dumb buffers were broken off on one side at both ends.

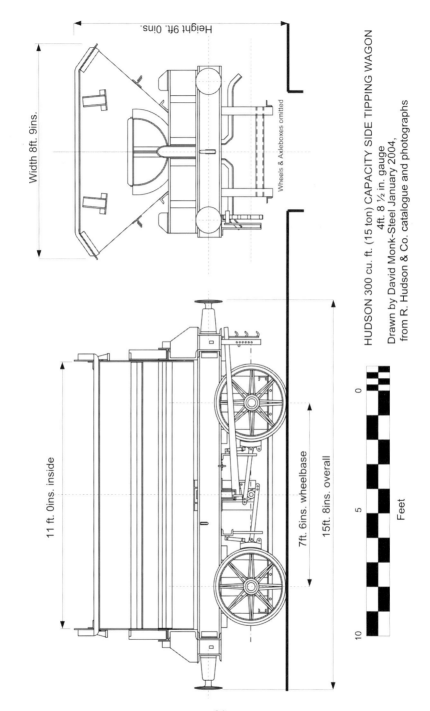

Width 8ft. 9ins.

Height 9ft. 0ins.

Wheels & Axleboxes omitted

11 ft. 0ins. inside

7ft. 6ins. wheelbase

15ft. 8ins. overall

HUDSON 300 cu. ft. (15 ton) CAPACITY SIDE TIPPING WAGON
4ft. 8 ½ in. gauge
Drawn by David Monk-Steel January 2004,
from R. Hudson & Co. catalogue and photographs

0

5

10

Feet

34

STEEL 15 TON TIPPING WAGON : NATIONAL COAL BOARD

(Brian Cuttell : 1993)

Builder – Robert Hudson & Co Ltd, Leeds

Date Built – not known

Length – 15ft 8in over buffers

Location – Booths Metals, Rotherham (awaiting scrap). Possibly originally used at one of the South or West Yorkshire collieries.

Livery – Originally, probably black with white lettering and 'St. Andrew's Cross'

Wheelbase – 7ft 6in

Height – 9ft 0in

Carrying capacity – 300cu yards, 15 tons

Purpose – removing mine stone to disposal

Fate – scrapped

Notes – the ubiquitous Hudson side tipping wagon was used extensively by civil engineering contractors and mines for the removal of spoil. Wagons of this type were also used for transporting clay, chalk and limestone from quarries to processing plant. Robert Hudson & Co advertised this wagon in many gauges and with variations to suit different operating conditions that might be encountered around the world. In the UK this type was typical.

IRONSTONE DUMP CAR : BSC CORBY (GRETTON BROOK)

(Author : 1990)

Builder – Metropolitan Carriage & Wagon Co Ltd

Date Built – 1940

Carrying capacity – 15 tons

Livery – rusty when seen, probably originally black

Location – originally Gretton Brook iron stone quarry in East Midlands; preserved at Rutland Railway Museum at Cottesmore in 1990

Length – 11ft 6in

Height – 7ft 6in

Wheelbase – 6ft 6in

Purpose – conveying iron stone from quarry to crushing plant

Fate – preserved at Cottesmore

Notes – wagons are based upon a North American 'dump car' design widely used for quarrying and construction work. These wagons were loaded by excavator and then locomotive hauled to the point of discharge where the body was tipped by hand. The action of tipping also caused the side door to rise away from the bodyside allowing the load to slide out freely. Rail clamps were provided to prevent the wagon falling over during discharge. The American influence was also apparent from the set of automatic couplers and the omission of side buffers. Versions of these wagons were built by a number of firms including Gloucester C & W Co and Metropolitan C & W Co.

SLUDGE TIPPING WAGON : YORKSHIRE WATER AUTHORITY

(Author : 1990)

Builder – Charles Roberts & Co Ltd, Horbury Junction, Wakefield

Date Built – 1961

Length – 21ft 0in over buffers

Wheelbase – 9ft 6in

Height – 9ft 4in

Carrying capacity – 420 cu ft

Location – Blackburn Meadows Sewage Works, Sheffield, now preserved at Rutland Railway Museum

Purpose – conveyance of sewage sludge 'cake' to disposal

Livery – red oxide

Fate – scrapped when rail traffic ceased, c1990, but this vehicle was preserved

Notes – for some years these vehicles also operated on BR metals to Thrybergh Tip, Rotherham. This wagon is an enlarged version of the standard side tipping wagon illustrated earlier, and has specially extended sides, to prevent loss of load when on the main line. For more information about these vehicles see *Industrial Railway Record* No.106.

BOGIE COIL WAGON – UES ROTHERHAM

(Author: 1995)

Builder – probably Birmingham Railway Carriage and Wagon Ltd, Birmingham

Date Built – unknown, probably 1950s

Length – about 36ft

Wheelbase – about 20ft bogie centres

Height – about 4ft 0in

Carrying capacity – approximately 75 tons

Location – based at Roundwood 11in Mill, Rotherham

Purpose – movement of rod coil within the Rotherham Works complex

Livery – yellow

Fate – still extant at Roundwood, 11in Mill (2004)

Notes – like many internal wagons it no longer carries maker's plates or inscriptions other than a number. It has stanchions and longitudinal bearers to support the load of coil. These vehicles were originally supplied to Steel, Peech and Tozer by BRCW for slab traffic from Templeborough to Brinsworth Strip Mill and were known as "Brinsworth Bogies".

It should be noted that the wagon depicted here is empty and is standing in front of rod coil stored on an elevated dispatch bay. A normal load for this wagon would be a single tier.

4 WHEEL WIRE COIL WAGON : UES ROTHERHAM

(Author : 1990)

Builder - built locally on chassis of former privately owned tank wagon

Date Built – unknown, probably 1970s

Length – 18ft 0in over headstocks

Wheelbase – 10ft 6in

Height – 5ft 6in

Carrying capacity – approximately 30 tons

Location – based at Roundwood 11" Mill site at Rotherham Works

Purpose – this is a specialised flat wagon provided to carry wire coil on the internal railway complex at Rotherham Works

Livery – red solebar but otherwise unpainted steel

Fate – probably still extant 2004

BOGIE OPEN WAGON : ALLIED STEEL AND WIRE CO. CARDIFF

(Trevor Mann : 1986)

Builder – converted by ASW on a former War Department Warflat chassis

Date Built – about 1942 for War Department; sold to Allied Steel and Wire and converted about 1985

Length – 40ft 0in over headstocks

Wheelbase – 30ft 0in bogie centres

Height – approximately 10ft 0in from rail

Carrying capacity – 50 tons

Location – Cardiff

Purpose – conveying scrap steel from scrap yard to melting shop

Livery – red with yellow and black wasp stripes at each end

Fate – cut down to flat wagon by 2000

4 WHEELED HEAVY SCRAP WAGON : BSC LACKENBY

(Peter Fidczuk : July 1989)

Builder – Standard Railway Wagon Co Ltd, Heywood, Lancashire

Date Built – uncertain, possibly about 1978

Length – approximately 20ft 0in

Wheelbase – approximately 12ft 0in

Height – approximately 12ft 0in

Carrying capacity – 55 tons

Location – Lackenby Steelworks, Cleveland

Purpose – conveyance of scrap steel within steelworks to the BOS steel plant

Livery – yellow with black solebars

Fate – believed scrapped or sold about 1995

Number series – HS2100 to HS2150

Notes – this vehicle numbered HS2148 was built by the Standard Wagon Co Ltd of Heywood in Lancashire and leased by the British Steel Corporation

GENERAL SERVICE WAGON : BSC RAVENSCRAIG

(Author : 1990)

Builder – unknown, probably BSC Ravenscraig on ex BR wagon chassis

Date Built – unknown

Length – 17ft 6in

Wheelbase – 10ft 0in

Height – approximately 6ft 6in from rail

Carrying capacity – unknown but probably about 20 tons

Location – BSC Ravenscraig Works, Motherwell

Purpose – transport of scrap steel from stockpile to melting shop

Livery – unpainted

Fate – not known, probably scrapped with the works on closure

Notes – this kind of wagon was typical of steel works rolling stock heavily rebuilt from older vehicles and designed for rough usage. Standard section and plate which would have been in plentiful supply and welded, bolted or riveted construction was used in the steelworks workshops to create a massive body that could withstand harsh and constant heavy contact with electro-magnet cranes and scrap metal.

OPEN MINERAL WAGON : NCB BRODSWORTH

(Author : 1987)

Builder – not known, registered by LNER E(30)5570, BR number P340560

Date Built – about 1930

Length – 16ft 6in

Wheelbase – 9ft 0 in

Height – approximately 8ft 0in

Carrying capacity – 12 tons

Location – Brodsworth, South Yorkshire

Purpose – transport of landsale coal in colliery complex

Livery – black with white lettering and IU stripes

Fate – scrapped on site

A.P.C.M. SWANCOMBE : CHALK TIPPLER WAGON

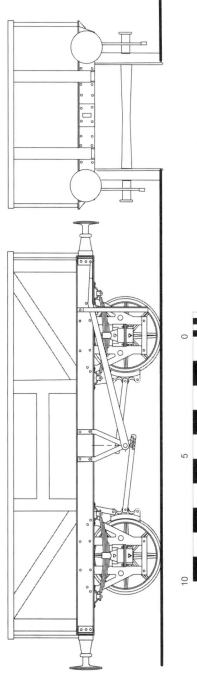

Drawn by David Monk-Steel from measurements taken by David Monk-Steel and Mark Saunders at North Downs Steam Railway, near Dartford

Body : 15ft 6in x 7ft 6in x 3ft 0in inside
wheelbase : 9ft 0in

Feet

0   5   10

Note that buffer heads are deliberately different diameters (13 in and 16 in) at either end of the wagon to avoid buffer-locking, the buffer guides as depicted are an earlier type drawn from information provided by APCM, and are not as fitted to the actual wagon measured. Note also the brake lever, blocks and hangar is provided on this side of the wagon only.

CHALK TIPPLER : APCM SWANSCOMBE

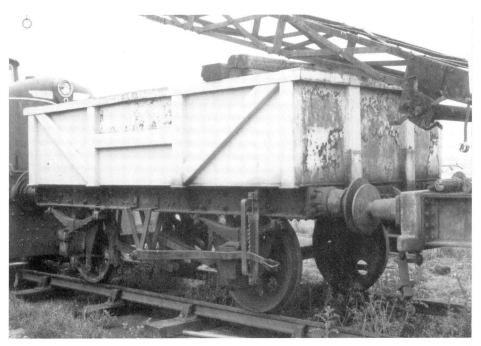

(Author : July 1992)

Builder – unknown but there is evidence that these vehicles were built in the West Midlands and transported to Kent over BR

Date Built – 1960s

Wheelbase – 9ft 0in

Length – 15ft 0in over headstocks

Height – inside of body – 3ft 0in, 6ft 10in rail to top

Carrying capacity – approximately 10 tons

Numbers – this is a sole survivor of 30 wagons built for the APCM Swanscombe on the chassis of wagons purchased from BR during the 1960s

Location – originally on the Blue Circle system, Swanscombe, Kent, subsequently preserved at Stone, near Dartford

Purpose – used to carry chalk from the quarry to the tippler at the cement works where the wagons were turned upside down to discharge the load

Livery – when delivered they were painted yellow with black lettering, but this soon weathered to white with a layer of chalk and cement dust

MINERAL OPEN WAGON : BATES COLLIERY BLYTH

(Collection of Mark Saunders)

Builder – uncertain, rebuilt with planked sides by NCB as a prototype, but not progressed

Date Built – about 1946

Length – 16ft 6in over headstocks

Wheelbase – 9ft 0in

Height – 8ft 9in approximately

Carrying capacity – 16 tons of coal

Location – at Bates Colliery, Northumberland in about 1978

Purpose – conveying coal from the washery to Bates Staiths

Livery – black with white lettering

Number series – 9177/243 to 9177/306 and 9252/1437 to 9252/1834 (some carried prefix 9185/--)

Fate – scrapped about 1982

Notes – this wagon is a former BR 16 ton Mineral Wagon that had been sold out of service to the NCB and has had the original sheeting and side doors replaced by timber planks because the original steel sheeting had corroded from the wet and acidic nature of the load. Timber was considered to be more resistant to this effect, and wooden rebodies had been carried out with some success in Durham but the fleet life expectancy was not considered great enough to continue this at Bates after this one prototype.

BOGIE OPEN WAGON : BSC WORKINGTON

(Author : 1984)

Builder – not known; converted from former War Department (World War 1) 'Warflat'

Date Built – about 1916

Length – 40ft 0in

Wheelbase – 30ft bogie centres

Height – approximately 6ft from rail

Carrying capacity – approximately 50 tons

Location – Workington

Purpose – in use conveying steel sleepers from the plant to the docks

Livery – originally red and black

Fate – scrapped about 1995

Notes – this open wagon was constructed using the chassis of a former War Department 'Warflat' wagon

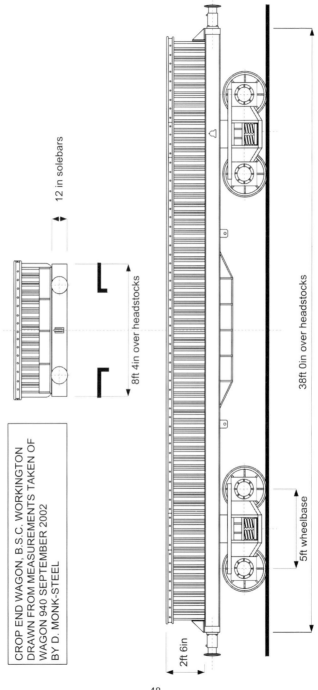

CROP END WAGON, B.S.C. WORKINGTON
DRAWN FROM MEASUREMENTS TAKEN OF
WAGON 940 SEPTEMBER 2002
BY D. MONK-STEEL

12 in solebars

8ft 4in over headstocks

38ft 0in over headstocks

5ft wheelbase

2ft 6in

48

BOGIE CROP END WAGON : BSC WORKINGTON

(Author : 1984)

Builder – Standard Wagon, Heywood, Lancashire

Date Built – not known

Length – 38ft 0in

Wheelbase – bogies 5ft 0in

Height – 6ft 3in from rail

Carrying capacity – 40 tons

Location – at BSC Workington in 1984

Purpose – originally for carrying pig iron discharged from a 'pig casting machine', latterly for scrap, cropped ends and general rubbish

Livery – unpainted

Fate – still in use (2003)

Notes -- this wagon is of massive construction designed to receive hot pigs from an automatic pig iron casting machine. It is made of bull head rails over a massive girder frame.

BOGIE OPEN WAGON : BSC WORKINGTON

(Author : 1984)

Builder – constructed locally on the chassis of a former War Department 'Warflat' type wagon

Date Built – unknown, chassis probably about 1916, rebuilt probably in the 1960s

Length – 40ft 0in over headstocks

Height – sides 13in high

Carrying capacity – approximately 45 tons

Livery – red timberwork and black steelwork

Numbers – this wagon is 955; others noted before 1994 were 951, 952 and 969

Location – BSC Workington

Purpose – to convey steel sleepers and other products to the docks from the steel works. Except within steelworks, bogie wagons in industrial service are not particularly numerous.

Note – typically of internal wagons this illustrated the diversity of rebuild when compared to the steel bodied variety

OPEN WAGON : ICI TUNSTEAD

(Author : March 1994)

Builder – not known

Date Built – not known

Length – 17ft 6in

Wheelbase – 10ft 0in

Height – 6ft 6in

Carrying capacity – 10 tons

Location – at ICI quarries Tunstead, Derbyshire

Purpose – originally for carrying lime, latterly used as a rubbish skip

Livery – originally yellow and grey, but heavily weathered light grey

Fate – probably scrapped

Notes – the vehicle is a former ICI Private Owner, being used internally within the Tunstead Quarry complex

OPEN WAGON : NCB LEA HALL

(Trevor Mann : 1986)

Builder – LMSR

Date Built – about 1926

Length – 16ft 6in

Wheelbase – 9ft 0in

Height – 8ft 6in

Carrying capacity – 12 tons

Location – Lea Hall Colliery in September 1986

Livery – black with white St. Andrew's cross and lettering

Purpose – conveying coal within the colliery system

Fate – scrapped or sold

Notes – National Coal Board open wagon number 287 formerly owned by the LMSR, diagram 1671, (Number M336663)

MEDIUM SIDED OPEN WAGON : NSF WINGERWORTH

(Author : 1985)

Builder – not known

Date Built – not known

Length – 15ft 9in over headstocks

Wheelbase – 9ft 0in

Height – 5ft 10¾in

Carrying capacity – 10 tons

Location – National Smokeless Fuels Ltd, Avenue Works, Wingerworth, Derbyshire

Purpose – general carriage in the works

Livery – unpainted

Fate – scrapped on site

Notes – a former Private Owner drop side wagon, for stone traffic (BR number P357135) in internal use

ENGINEERING WAGON : TYNE & WEAR METRO

(David Ratcliffe : 1987)

Builder – Procor, Horbury Junction, Wakefield

Date Built – 1977

Length – 62ft 4in

Wheelbase – 46ft 11in bogie centres

Height – 12 ft approximately from rail

Carrying capacity – nil

Location – South Gosforth

Purpose – maintenance access to overhead power cables

Livery – black with 'Metro' insignia on a yellow patch

Fate – extant

Notes – originally registered for operating over BR lines. In practice these vehicles operated internally over the Tyne & Wear Metro system, and are used as working platforms during repairs to the overhead power lines.

BREAKDOWN TOOL VAN : NCB DERWENTHAUGH

(Author : 1984)

Builder – probably constructed locally using parts of a former coal wagon

Date Built – unknown

Length – approximately 15ft 0in over headstocks

Wheelbase – 9ft 0in

Height – approximately 9ft

Carrying capacity – not known, used for tools and packing

Location – Derwenthaugh Coke Ovens, Co.Durham 1986

Purpose – many private systems had vehicles in which jacks, tools and packing material could be kept secure and carried to the site of a derailment. This van was used for this purpose. Note the brake lever in the obsolete left handed position.

Livery – red with white lettering and edges to the step boards

Fate – scrapped on site 1986

TOOLVAN : ALLIED STEEL & WIRE CARDIFF

(Author : 1999)

Builder – Swindon BR (W)

Date Built – 1948, as W35377 – purchased 1994

Length – 24ft 0in over headstocks

Wheelbase – 16ft 0in

Height – 11ft 1¾in to top of roof

Carrying capacity – not applicable

Location – ASW Tremorfa Works, Cardiff

Purpose – transporting re-railing gear to site, and crew accommodation

Livery – yellow with wasp stripes

Fate – extant

Notes – Number RR1. Works with plate wagon RR2 formerly LC738 (ex BR Coil E - B933252).

CABLE REEL WAGON : BOWES RAILWAY

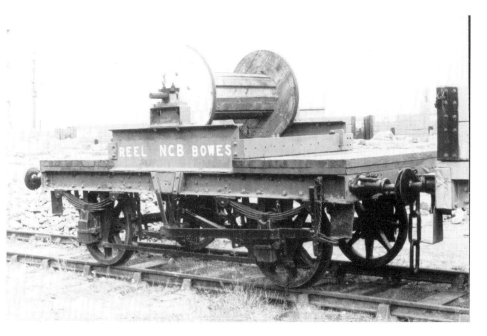

(Author : 1991)

Builder – Darlington Wagon & Engineering Co Ltd, rebuilt by Bowes Railway, Springwell Wagon Shops

Date Built – originally about 1887

Length – 14ft 10in approximately

Wheelbase – 9ft 0in

Carrying capacity – originally 10 tons

Location – Bowes Railway, Springwell in 1987

Purpose – a specially converted vehicle for paying out new haulage cables on the inclines of the Bowes Railway

Livery – red with black iron work and white lettering

Notes – this wagon is built on the chassis of a former 10 ton coal wagon

Fate – preserved at Springwell, it is still used for its originally designed purpose

ADAPTOR WAGON FOR INGOT BOGIES : BSC SCUNTHORPE

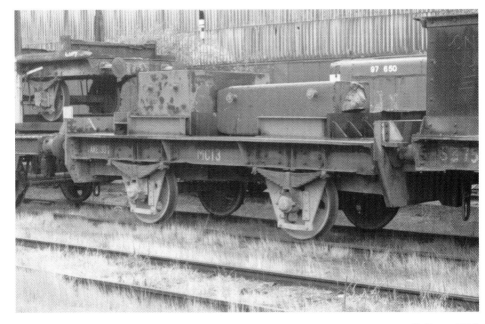

(Author : 1984)

Builder – unknown

Date Built – unknown

Length – approximately 18ft 0in

Wheelbase – approximately 10ft 0in

Height – approximately 6ft 0in

Carrying capacity – not applicable, tare weight 30 tons

Location – at Scunthorpe 10/1994

Purpose – incorporates semi automatic adaptor couplings to attach ingot bogie cars to a locomotive, and to provide some spacing between ingot bogies and the locomotive crew when trains of hot ingots are being worked

Livery – unpainted (other wagons of this type were painted yellow)

Fate – believed still in use

TEST WEIGHT WAGON : UES ALDWARKE

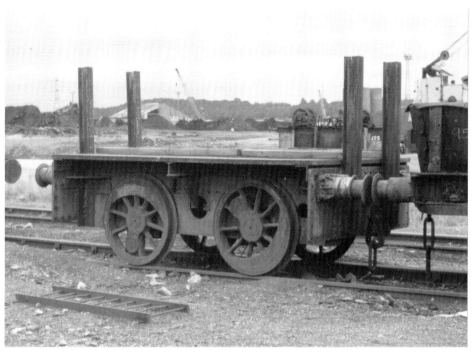

(Author : 1994)

Builder – Steel, Peech & Tozer Ltd, Rotherham

Date Built – 1961 (converted from chassis of steam locomotive RSH7020/1941)

Length – approximately 8ft 0in

Wheelbase – approximately 5ft 6in

Height – approximately 4ft 0in

Carrying capacity – not known, probably 30 tons

Location – United Engineering Steels, Rotherham Works

Purpose – weighbridge testing

Livery – black/unpainted

Fate – scrapped

Notes – originally at Steel, Peech & Tozer's works

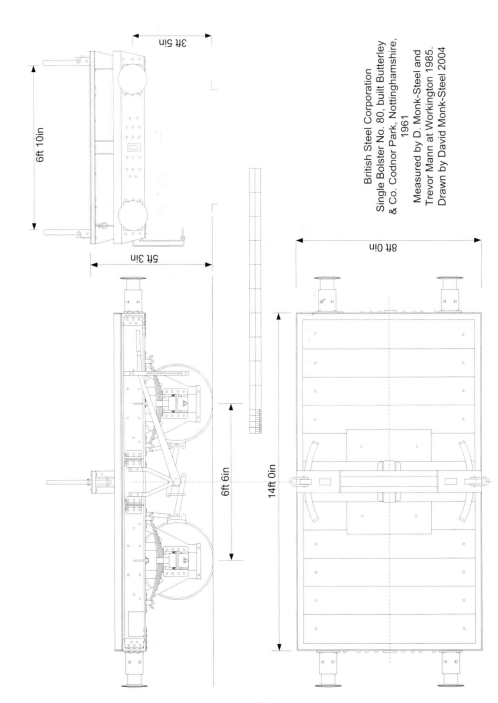

British Steel Corporation
Single Bolster No. 80, built Butterley
& Co. Codnor Park, Nottinghamshire,
1961
Measured by D. Monk-Steel and
Trevor Mann at Workington 1985.
Drawn by David Monk-Steel 2004

3ft 5in

6ft 10in

5ft 3in

14ft 0in

6ft 6in

8ft 0in

SINGLE BOLSTER : BSC WORKINGTON

(Author : 1984)

Builder – Standard Railway Wagon Co Ltd, Heywood, Lancashire

Date Built – about 1966

Length – 14ft 0in over headstocks

Wheelbase – 6ft 6in

Height – 5ft 3in to top of bolster

Carrying capacity – about 20 tons

Location – Workington, Cumbria

Purpose – transport of rails from the rolling mills to Workington Docks

Livery – black

Fate – a few extant but not used for original purposes

Notes – originally this was a fleet of about 120 vehicles but all have now been superseded by bogie bolsters purchased second hand from BR

INGOT BOGIE : UES STOCKSBRIDGE

(Author : 1994)

Builder – Bolton Railway Wagon and Ironworks

Date Built – not known, possibly 1956

Length – 16ft 2in over headstocks

Wheelbase – 8ft 0in

Height – 3ft 6in approximately

Carrying capacity – approximately 50 – 60 tons

Location – Stocksbridge Engineering Steels, Stocksbridge, South Yorkshire

Purpose – conveying steel ingots from melting shop or stockpile to the rolling mill

Livery – unpainted

Fate – many still extant and in use (2004)

Notes – bogie is reported to have been transferred from BSC Bilston Works, West Midlands

FUEL OIL TANK WAGON : NCB HAWTHORN MINE

(Mark Saunders : 1991)

Builder – constructed by the NCB on the chassis of a former 14 ton coal hopper wagon

Date Built – unknown, probably in 1970s

Length – 16ft 6in

Wheelbase – 10ft 6in

Height – approximately 10 ft

Carrying capacity – 6500 litres

Location – Hawthorn Mine, near Seaham, County Durham in November 1991

Purpose – a tank wagon was in use to supply gas oil (diesel) to mobile plant working on the surface

Livery – black or very dark green, yellow lettering and stripes

Fate – preserved at the Bowes Railway, Springwell, Co. Durham

CYLINDRICAL TANK : BSC RAVENSCRAIG

(Author : 1990)

Builder – probably Charles Roberts & Co Ltd

Date Built – about 1958

Length – 23ft 8½in over headstocks

Wheelbase – 15ft 0in

Height – 12ft 4½in overall

Carrying capacity – 22tons 10cwt

Location – BSC Ravenscraig Works, Motherwell

Purpose – coke oven wash oil store

Livery – black

Fate – scrapped

Notes – this wagon appears to have been formerly a class 'B' tank wagon, probably originally hired from E.G. Steele by Scottish Agricultural Industries

NITRIC ACID TANK : MOD BISHOPTON

(Greg Martin : 1991)

Builder – Charles Roberts & Co Ltd

Date Built – about 1941

Length –16ft 6in over headstocks

Wheelbase – 9ft 0in

Height – approximately 9ft 9in

Carrying capacity – 14 tons

Location – Bishopton

Purpose – storage and conveyance of nitric acid within the plant

Livery – black

Fate – probably scrapped

Notes – formerly a private owner wagon registered by GWR (421/1941) to operate over the main lines

RECTANGULAR TANK : YTD KILNHURST

(Author : 1984)

Builder – not known

Date Built – not known

Length –16ft 6in over headstocks

Wheelbase – 9ft 0in

Height – about 8ft 0in to top of tank

Carrying capacity – about 12 tons

Location – Yorkshire Tar Distillers, Kilnhurst, South Yorkshire

Purpose – storage of tar products on site

Livery – black

Fate – scrapped

Notes – formerly a private owner tank wagon registered to operate over main lines. Registration plates and builders plates have been removed.

MANGANESE HOPPER : BSC TEESSIDE

(Author : 1985)

Builder – Head Wrightson & Co Ltd

Built – 1950s

Length – approximately 21 ft over headstocks

Wheelbase – approximately 15 ft

Height – approximately 10 ft

Carrying capacity – 45 tons

Location – BSC Teesside, North Yorkshire

Purpose – transport of manganese ore from Tees Docks and stockpile to the "Bessemer" blast furnaces at Cleveland Works

Livery – grey

Fate – scrapped

Notes – observed in 1985 but are no longer used at the plant

WEIGHTS VAN : NCB ASHINGTON

(Author : 1985)

Builder – North Eastern Railway

Date Built – before 1891

Length – 15ft 10in approximately

Wheelbase – 9ft 6in approximately

Height –10ft 0in approximately

Carrying capacity – 8 tons

Location – NCB Ashington

Purpose – carrying test weights for weighbridge testing

Livery – black with white lettering

Fate – scrapped about 1985

PALVAN : MOD MARCHWOOD

(Greg Martin : 1993)

Builder – British Railways Wolverton to Lot No.3392, originally BR No. B781861

Date Built – 1960

Length – 17ft 6in over headstocks

Wheelbase – 10ft 0in

Height – 11ft 8in approximately

Carrying capacity – 12 tons

Location – Marchwood

Purpose – conveying stores within the site

Livery – dark green with black solebars and underframe

Fate – scrapped or sold

Notes – it was subsequently sold to the MOD for internal use at Marchwood and repainted and re-numbered WGB4255. Other numbers included WGB 4259, 4260, 4275, 4276, 4279 to 4283.

GUNPOWDER VAN : ADMIRALTY

(A.R. Etherington)

Builder – not known

Date Built – not known

Length – 9ft

Wheelbase – 4ft 9in (2ft 4in diameter wheels)

Height – body 4ft 11in at side, approximately 7ft 9in from rail to top of roof

Carrying capacity – approximately 4 tons

Location – in preservation at Shackerstone

Purpose – conveyance of explosives

Livery – grey

Fate – extant at Shackerstone

Notes – the gunpowder van, which was photographed at Shackerstone in 12/2004, was originally operated at the RNAD depot at Bedenham and makes an interesting comparison with the 'standard' box van behind it

BOGIE WELL WAGON : BSC WORKINGTON

(Author : 1984)

Builder – unknown, possibly British Steel

Date Built – unknown

Length – approximately 30ft 0ins over headstocks

Bogie Wheelbase – 5 ft 0ins

Height – approximately 1ft 6in in the well

Carrying capacity – about 40 tons

Location – at British Steel, Workington in 1984

Purpose – it is possible that it was used to convey plant and machinery in the steelworks complex

Livery – unpainted

Fate – extant and in use January 1984, scrapped or sold by 1990

Notes – the precise purpose of this wagon is unknown, but see note above

.

FLAT TROLLEY WAGON : BSC CORBY

(Author : 1990)

Builder – Head Wrightson & Co Ltd

Date Built – 1950s

Length – about 35ft

Wheelbase – 5ft 6in bogies

Height – about 1ft 6in in well

Carrying capacity – 40 tons

Location – Cottesmore in 1990, formerly at BSC Corby

Purpose – conveying plant and machinery, especially excavators, in the ironstone quarry system

Livery – grey

Fate – preserved at the Rutland Railway Museum

Notes – note the trestle for carrying the crane jib. Despite being listed in the museum catalogue as a former main line wagon it is identical to a vehicle illustrated in a 1950s Head Wrightson catalogue for a private customer for the carriage of excavators, and bears no similarity to any known main line designs.

FLAT TROLLEY WAGON : UES STOCKSBRIDGE

(Author : 1994)

Builder – unknown

Date Built – before 1923, reportedly arrived here from Scunthorpe

Length – over headstocks, 28ft 0in

Wheelbase – 22ft 0in

Height – 1ft 6in approximately

Carrying capacity – unknown, probably 20 tons

Location – Stocksbridge Engineering Steels, Stocksbridge, South Yorkshire

Purpose – machinery transport

Livery – unpainted

Fate – scrapped or sold by 2003

Notes – it is uncertain if this is an ex BR wagon or a steel company copy. Although it has a number of features of a LNER vehicle it is unlike any illustrated in the LNER diagram book and bears no evidence of main line use. It may have been purpose built for the Stocksbridge Railway Company but this is purely conjecture. Measurements are estimated.

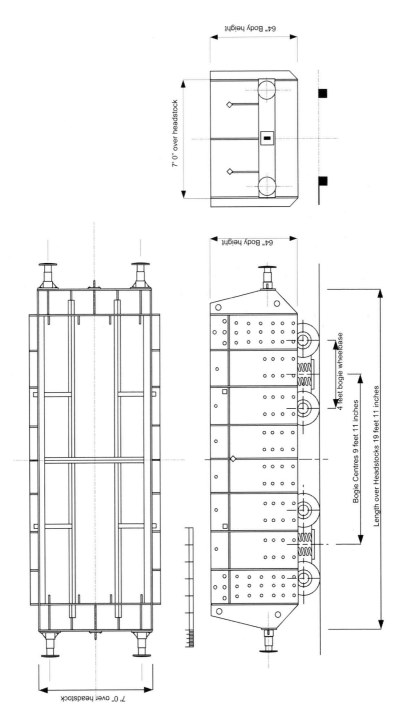

64" Body height

7' 0" over headstock

64" Body height

4 feet bogie wheelbase

Bogie Centres 9 feet 11 inches

Length over Headstocks 19 feet 11 inches

7' 0" over headstock

74

BOGIE HOT INGOT CAR : UES STOCKSBRIDGE

(Author : 1995)

Builder – not known, transferred here from Corby in 1981

Date Built – not known, probably mid-1960s

Length – 19ft 11in over headstocks

Wheelbase – 13 ft 10in

Height – 5ft 4in sides

Carrying capacity – 37.5 tons

Location – at Stocksbridge Steel Works, Stocksbridge, South Yorkshire

Purpose – transferring hot ingots from melting shop to rolling mill

Livery – unpainted

Fate – still in service (2004)

Notes – known locally as 'Panzers'; ten vehicles on site (Nos. 1,3 to 11)

BOGIE HOT METAL TORPEDO WAGON : BSC TEESSIDE

(Author : 1986)

Builder – Distington Engineering to a Demag design

Date Built – 1975

Length – 27 metres

Wheelbase – 25 metres approximately

Height – 4.25 metres

Carrying capacity – 300 tons

Location – Teesside Iron and Steelworks complex

Purpose – transport of molten iron, between the Blast Furnace at Tod Point Redcar, and the Steelworks at Lackenby. Often worked in sets of two (loaded) or three (empty).

Livery – black and yellow where painted

Fate – at least 12 were still in service in 1991; probably all still in use (2004)

Notes – essentially a German design on 16 axles. Molten iron is poured into the opening at the top of the centre of the ladle, and is discharged into a receiving vessel or pit by rotating the entire ladle by remote control. The worn refractory lining is replaced, once cooled, by removing the end caps.

BOGIE INGOT CASTING CAR : BSC SCUNTHORPE

(Author : 1994)

Builder – Head Wrightson & Co Ltd

Date Built – 1971

Length – 24ft 7in

Wheelbase – 17ft 10in

Height – 3ft 6in

Carrying capacity – 50 tons

Location – Scunthorpe

Purpose – molten steel is teemed into moulds mounted on the casting cars; after solidification the still hot ingots are transferred on the bogies from the steel plant to the rolling mills. At most works the moulds were stripped off the ingots at the melting shop, but at some the moulds remained on the car for the journey to the rolling mill.

Livery – unpainted

Fate – most, if not all, scrapped. The casting of ingots on locomotive-hauled bogies at Scunthorpe ceased about 2000.

BOGIE HOT METAL TORPEDO CAR : BSC RAVENSCRAIG

(Author :1994)

Builder – Ashmore, Benson Pease & Co Ltd

Date Built – not known

Length – about 70 feet

Wheelbase – four bogies with 5ft 6in wheelbase

Height – about 14 feet

Carrying capacity – 150 tons

Location – Ravenscraig

Purpose – Torpedo car for internal movement of liquid iron from the blast furnaces to BOS steel plant

Livery – unpainted

Fate – scrapped

Notes – eleven cars of this design numbered 1 to 7 and 10 to 13 were on hand when the plant closed, together with four cars built by Distington to a slightly different design (numbered 14, 16, 19 and 20)

BOGIE SLAG LADLE : POLLOCK TYPE : BSC RAVENSCRAIG

(Author : 1994)

Builder – Ashmore, Benson, Pease & Co Ltd

Date Built – 1970s

Length – 18ft 1in over headstocks

Wheelbase – 16ft 10in

Height – 9ft 8in

Carrying capacity – 40 tons

Location – BSC Ravenscraig Works, Motherwell

Purpose – removing molten slag tapped from blast furnaces to the slag bank for disposal

Livery – unpainted

Fate – scrapped

Notes – the ladle is tipped by remote control using an air cylinder engine mounted on the wagon. One similar vehicle is preserved near Redcar.

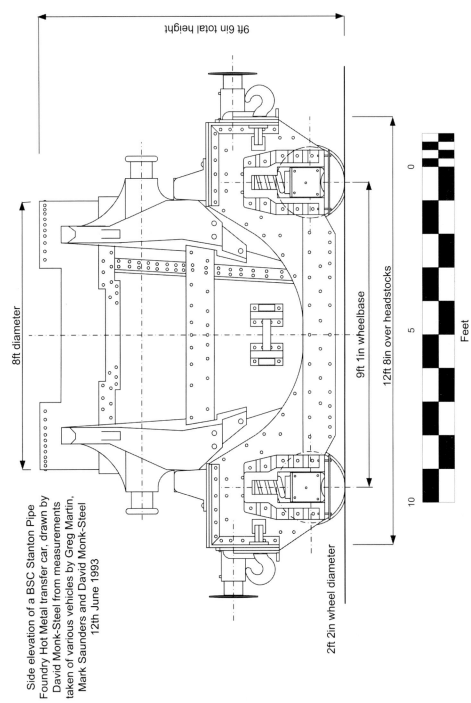

9ft 6in total height

8ft diameter

9ft 1in wheelbase

12ft 8in over headstocks

2ft 2in wheel diameter

Side elevation of a BSC Stanton Pipe
Foundry Hot Metal transfer car, drawn by
David Monk-Steel from measurements
taken of various vehicles by Greg Martin,
Mark Saunders and David Monk-Steel
12th June 1993

0

5

10

Feet

80

MOLTEN METAL LADLE CAR : STANTON IRONWORKS

(Author : 1995)

Builder – unknown

Date Built – unknown

Length – 12ft 8in over headstocks

Wheelbase – 9ft 1in

Height – 10ft to top of ladle

Carrying capacity – about 30 tons

Location – BSC Stanton Ironworks

Purpose – transport of molten iron within Stanton Works complex from melting shop to pipe foundry

Livery – unpainted

Fate – unknown, probably still in service with St. Gobains Pipelines at Stanton

BOGIE HOT METAL LADLE TRANSFER CAR : BSC CONSETT

(Author : 1986)

Builder – not known

Date Built – not known

Wheelbase – 21ft 6in

Length – 24ft 5in

Height – 11ft 5in to top of ladle

Location – Consett, Co. Durham

Carrying capacity – about 40 tons

Purpose – transferring iron from the blast furnaces to steel plant

Livery – black and yellow where painted

Fate – having survived the demolition of the Consett Works complex that had closed in 1980, this and another larger ladle transfer car were stored in the car park of the Resident Engineer for the scheme to reclaim the site. Together with a third similar vehicle they were later stored alongside the long distance cycle path at Lounds Gill and then transformed into an industrial work of art.

Notes – transfer cars of this type were used at integrated steel works. The ladle would be filled with molten iron at the blast furnace, then moved to the steel plant where the ladle only would be transferred by overhead cranes within the shop. The cars were of massive construction to resist the extreme conditions in which they operated. The sloping ends were protected from iron spillage by a layer of firebrick.

BOGIE COKE DUMP CAR : NSF WINGERWORTH

(Author : 1987)

Builder – not known

Date Built – not known

Length – 50ft 0in hopper

Wheelbase – about 40 ft

Height – typically 15ft 3in

Carrying capacity – 2200 cu ft of hot coke

Location – National Smokeless Fuels, Avenue Works, Wingerworth, Derbyshire

Purpose – receiving red hot coke from the coke ovens, and transporting it firstly into a quenching tower (where the coke was cooled with a water douche) and then to a discharging pit (where the cooled coke was cascaded for collection either by a conveyor or by shovels and wagons)

Livery – black

Fate – scrapped

Note – each coke car was semi-permanently coupled to a locomotive, usually electrically propelled, that incorporated air control equipment for operating the coke discharge doors and in some cases body tipping mechanism as well

INGOT FLAT WAGON : ESC SHEFFIELD

(Head Wrightson & Co Ltd)

Builder – Head, Wrightson & Co (for English Steel Corporation)

Date Built – 1940s

Length – about 70ft

Wheelbase – about 62ft

Height – about 8ft rail to platform

Carrying capacity – 300 tons

Location – River Don Works, Sheffield (ESC, later BSC)

Purpose – convey heavy cast steel ingots within the River Don Works complex. Also used occasionally to transfer such ingots (each weighing in excess of 200 tonnes) between River Don Works and nearby Grimesthorpe Works over BR metals.

Livery – grey

Fate – scrapped in late 1980s

Note – this was a very large wagon, and had the greatest carrying capacity of any single vehicle on a British railway system at the time. It is understood that it was set aside after rail traffic ceased in case the National Railway Museum was interested in preserving it, but in the end it was broken up.

SELECTED INDUSTRIAL SITES RECORDED SINCE 1980

The following locations are known to have internal wagon fleets of significant size and/or interest

Area	County	Firm	Address	Wagons	Note
Cumbria & North West	Cumbria	National Coal Board	Haig Colliery	Hopper wagons, mineral wagons	Closed
Cumbria and North West	Cumbria	British Nuclear Fuels PLC.	Sellafield,	Nuclear flask transporters, tank wagons, specially constructed well wagons	Still operating 2003
Cumbria and North West	Cumbria	Corus (formerly British Steel)	Moss Bay Steelworks, Workington	Bogie bolsters, single bolsters, flat wagons, general service and open wagons, crop end wagons and roll wagons	Still operating 2004
Cumbria and North West	Cumbria	Ministry of Defence, Army Department	Longtown Depot, Carlisle	Vans, high opens, medium opens, palvans, tank wagon (ex DR), brake van	Last reported 1994
East Midlands	Leicestershire	National Coal Board	Rawdon Colliery	Mineral wagons	Closed
East Midlands	Northamptonshire	British Steel	Corby Works	Tube wagons, open wagons	Internal rail traffic ceased
Eastern Counties	Cambridgeshire	Rugby Cement	Barrington Cement Works,	Chalk and clay tipper wagons	Still operating 2004
Eastern Counties	Essex	Ministry of Defence, Army Department	Shoeburyness	Vans, flat wagons, bogie flat wagons, bogie well wagons	Last reported 1993
Home Counties North	Buckinghamshire	Castle Cement (form. Tunnel Cement)	Pitstone, near Tring	Chalk tipper wagons (incl. Ex BR iron ore tipplers)	Closed; last reported 1991
Home Counties South	Hampshire	Ministry of Defence, Army Department	Marchwood Depot	Pallet vans, Warflats, Warwells.	Last reported 1993

SELECTED INDUSTRIAL SITES RECORDED SINCE 1980

The following locations are known to have internal wagon fleets of significant size and/or interest

Area	County	Firm	Address	Wagons	Note
Home Counties South	Hampshire	Ministry of Defence, Navy Department	Bedenham (Gosport)	Vans, open wagons, pipe wagons, flat wagons	Last report 1993
Home Counties South	Kent	Blue Circle	Swanscombe	Flat wagons, chalk tippler wagons	Closed
Home Counties South	Kent	Reed Paper & Board (UK) Ltd	Empire Paper Mills, Greenhithe	Flat wagons	Closed
Home Counties South	Kent	Sheerness Iron & Steel Co Ltd	Sheerness	Open wagons, bogie bolsters	Rail traffic ceased
London		Ford Motor Company	Dagenham Works	Flat wagons, open wagons, scrap wagons	Last reported 1988
London		London Underground	Neasden, Lillie Bridge Acton, Ruislip etc,	Bogie flat wagons, bogie hopper wagons, cable drum wagons, bogie open wagons	still operating 2003
London		Purfleet Deep Water Wharf & Storage Co	Erith Wharf	Flat wagons, open wagons	Closed about 1983
North East	Cleveland	Corus (formerly British Steel)	Teesside Works, Cleveland	Torpedo ladles, slag ladles, ingot bogies, heavy and light scrap wagons, tippler wagons, bogie bolsters, flat wagons, coil wagons, hopper wagons, coke cars	Still operating 2004 but with reduced fleet
North East	Cleveland	T.J. Thompson	Millfield Works, Stockton, Cleveland	Open wagons, mineral wagons flat wagons	Still operating 2003
North East	Cleveland	Tees and Hartlepool Port Authority	Tees Dock, Middlesbrough	Bogie bolsters, flat wagons	Closed

SELECTED INDUSTRIAL SITES RECORDED SINCE 1980

The following locations are known to have internal wagon fleets of significant size and/or interest

Area	County	Firm	Address	Wagons	Note
North East	Co.Durham	British Steel	Consett Steelworks	Hot metal ladles, slag ladles, open wagons, hopper wagons	Closed in 1980
North East	Co.Durham	National Coal Board	Hawthorn Mine, South Hetton	Coal hopper wagons	Closed about 1989
North East	Co.Durham	National Coal Board	Easington Colliery	Coal hopper wagons	Closed about 1988
North East	Co.Durham	National Coal Board	Seaham Colliery	Coal hopper wagons	Closed about 1988
North East	Co Durham	National Coal Board	Dawdon Colliery, Seaham	Coal hopper wagons	Closed
North East	Co.Durham	National Coal Board	Horden Colliery	Coal hopper wagons	Closed
North East	Northumberland	National Coal Board	Bates Colliery, Blyth	Mineral open wagons	Closed about 1985
North East	Northumberland	National Coal Board	Weetslade Washery, Killingworth	Coal hopper wagons	Closed about 1985
North East	Northumberland	National Coal Board	Ashington Colliery, Ashington	Coal hopper wagons	Closed about 1986
North East	Northumberland	National Coal Board	Whittle Colliery, Newton on the Moor	Coal hopper wagons	Closed
North East	Tyne & Wear	Tyne & Wear PTE	Gosforth	Bogie flat wagons, bogie hopper wagons, cable drum wagons, bogie open wagons	Still operating 2003
North East	Tyne & Wear	National Coal Board	Westoe Colliery, South Shields	Coal hopper wagons	Closed about 1988

SELECTED INDUSTRIAL SITES RECORDED SINCE 1980

The following locations are known to have internal wagon fleets of significant size and/or interest

Area	County	Firm	Address	Wagons	Note
North East	Tyne & Wear	National Smokeless Fuels Ltd	Derwenthaugh Coke Works, Swalwell	Coal hopper wagons, tank wagons, coke car	Closed about 1986
Scotland	Strathclyde	British Steel	Ravenscraig, Motherwell	Torpedo ladles, Pollock ladles, coke cars, bogie bolsters, general service and scrap carrying wagons	Closed by 1994
Scotland	Strathclyde	Ministry of Defence, Royal Ordnance Factory	Bishopton	Tank wagons, vans	Closed about 1991
Scotland	Fife	Ministry of Defence, Navy Department	Rosyth	Open wagons, bogie plate wagon	Last reported 1986
South West	Avon	Port of Bristol Authority	Avonmouth Docks	Open wagons, vans	Stock sold
South West	Avon	Port of Bristol Authority	Bristol Docks	Open wagons, flat wagons, van, tank wagons, bogie well wagon	Last reported 1992 (possibly preserved stock)
South West	Devon	Ministry of Defence, Navy Department	Armament Depot, Ernsettle		
South West	Somerset	Ministry of Defence, Royal Ordnance Factory	Puriton	Tank wagons, vans, iron ore hoppers, steel mineral wagons	Last reported 1991
Wales North	Clwyd	British Steel	Shotton	Only narrow gauge wagons reported in recent years.	Standard gauge closed
Wales North	Clywd	United Engineering Steels (formerly GKN)	Brymbo Steelworks	Hopper wagons, side tipping wagons, pig iron basket wagons, hot metal ladles, slag ladles, bogie bolsters	Closed
Wales South	Dyfed	Duport Steels Ltd	Llanelli	?	Closed

SELECTED INDUSTRIAL SITES RECORDED SINCE 1980

The following locations are known to have internal wagon fleets of significant size and/or interest

Area	County	Firm	Address	Wagons	Note
Wales South	Dyfed	Ministry of Defence, Army Department	RNAD, Milford Haven	?	
Wales South	Gwent	Corus, (formerly British Steel)	Ebbw Vale	?	Closed
Wales South	Gwent	Corus Strip Products, (formerly British Steel)	Llanwern	?	No rolling stock reports received, but works still open 2004.
Wales South	South Glamorgan	Allied Steel & Wire	Castle & Tremorfa Works, Cardiff	Coil wagons, bolster wagons, bogie bolster wagons, scrap open wagons,	Still operating 2003, but reported subsequently closed.
Wales South	West Glamorgan	Corus, Strip Products, (formerly British Steel)	Port Talbot	Torpedo ladles	Still operating 2004
Welsh Marches	Herefordshire	Ministry of Defence, Army Department	Moreton-on-Lugg		
West Midlands	Oxfordshire	Ministry of Defence, Army Department	Bicester	Vans, bogie flat wagons, open wagons	Last reported 1990
West Midlands	Staffordshire	British Steel	Shelton, Etruria, Stoke	Bogie bolster wagons, flat wagons,	Closed (last report 1994)
West Midlands	Warwickshire	Ministry of Defence, Army Department	Kineton Depot	Warflat, bogie flat (other). Note this depot has been used for secure storage for rolling stock of main line companies	Last reported 1997
West Midlands	Warwickshire	Ministry of Defence, Army Department	Long Marston Depot	Open wagons, vans, flat wagons, tank wagon.	Last reported 1986

89

SELECTED INDUSTRIAL SITES RECORDED SINCE 1980

The following locations are known to have internal wagon fleets of significant size and/or interest

Area	County	Firm	Address	Wagons	Note
West Midlands	West Midlands	Austin Rover Group Ltd	Longbridge Works, Birmingham	Mineral wagons	Closed
West Midlands	West Midlands	British Steel	Bilston Steelworks		Closed
West Midlands	West Midlands	National Coal Board	Coventry Colliery, Keresley	Mineral wagons	Closed
West Midlands	West Midlands	National Smokeless Fuels Ltd.	Homefire Plant, Keresley	Mineral wagons, coke car	
West Midlands	West Midlands	Round Oak Steel Works Ltd	Brierley Hill		Closed
North Midlands	Derbyshire	(Tube Investments) Chesterfield Cylinders	Chesterfield	Tube wagon, pipe wagon, open wagons	Rail traffic ceased
North Midlands	Derbyshire	Coalite Ltd.	Bolsover Works, Buttermilk Lane, Bolsover	Hopper wagons, mineral wagons	Fleet reduced but still operating 2003, subsequently closed
North Midlands	Derbyshire	ICI Industries	Tunstead Limeworks and Quarries	Open wagons, tank wagons (cut down to open wagons)	Still operating 2003
North Midlands	Derbyshire	National Coal Board	Cadley Hill Colliery	Mineral wagons	Closed
North Midlands	Derbyshire	National Smokeless Fuels Ltd.	Avenue Carbonisation Plant, Wingerworth	Coke car, tank wagons, hopper wagons, open wagons	Closed
North Midlands	Derbyshire	British Steel	Staveley Works, Barrow Hill, Staveley	Open wagons, mineral wagons	Rail traffic ceased

SELECTED INDUSTRIAL SITES RECORDED SINCE 1980

The following locations are known to have internal wagon fleets of significant size and/or interest

Area	County	Firm	Address	Wagons	Note
North Midlands	Derbyshire	St. Gobain Pipelines (formerly British Steel)	Stanton Works, Ilkeston	Hot metal (liquid iron) ladle wagons	Still operating 2004
Eastern England	North Lincolnshire	Corus, (formerly British Steel)	Scunthorpe Steelworks, Brigg Road. Scunthorpe	Torpedo ladles, slag ladles, ingot bogies, general service and scrap wagons, tippler wagons, bogie section wagons, bogie bolsters, flat wagons, coil wagons, roll wagons, hopper wagons, coke cars	Still operating 2004; some wagons are also preserved on site
East Midlands	Nottinghamshire	National Coal Board	Sutton in Ashfield	Mineral wagons	Closed
Yorks	North Yorkshire	British Oil & Cake Mills	Olympia Works, Selby	Covered hopper wagons	Still operating 2003
Yorks	South Yorkshire	Corus, (formerly British Steel)	Rotherham Works complex, Aldwarke Roundwood and Thrybergh	Bogie bolsters, twin bolsters, flat wagons, coil wagons, general service and scrap wagons, and tank wagons.	Still operating 2004
Yorks	South Yorkshire	Corus, (formerly British Steel)	Stocksbridge Steelworks	Bogie bolsters, twin bolsters, flat wagons, ingot and bloom wagons, general service and scrap wagons,	Still operating 2004
Yorks	South Yorkshire	British Steel	River Don Works, Sheffield	Flat wagons	Rail traffic ceased 1986
Yorks	South Yorkshire	United Engineering Steels	Templeborough Works, Ickles, Rotherham	Bogie bolsters, twin bolsters, flat wagons, general service and scrap wagons,	Closed 1993
Yorks	South Yorkshire	British Steel	BSC Chemicals, Orgreave Cokeworks, Sheffield	Mineral wagons, hopper wagons, coke car, tank wagons	Closed 1988
Yorks	South Yorkshire	Coalite Ltd	Askern, Doncaster	Hopper wagons, mineral wagons	Closed

91

SELECTED INDUSTRIAL SITES RECORDED SINCE 1980

The following locations are known to have internal wagon fleets of significant size and/or interest

Area	County	Firm	Address	Wagons	Note
Yorks	South Yorkshire	Coalite Ltd	Grimethorpe, near Barnsley	Hopper wagons, mineral wagons	Closed, last reported 1988
Yorks	South Yorkshire	Croda Hydrocarbons (formerly Yorkshire Tar Distillers Ltd)	Kilnhurst	Tank wagons	Closed
Yorks	South Yorkshire	Hadfields Ltd	Attercliffe, Sheffield	Open wagons, flat wagons, tank wagons (cut down to open wagons)	Closed
Yorks	South Yorkshire	National Coal Board	Brodsworth Colliery, Woodlands	Hopper wagons, mineral wagons	Closed, last reported 1987
Yorks	South Yorkshire	National Coal Board	Manvers and Barnborough Collieries, Wath upon Dearne	Hopper wagons, mineral wagons	Closed, last reported 1988
Yorks	South Yorkshire	National Coal Board	Cadeby Colliery, Conisborough	Mineral wagons	Closed
Yorks	South Yorkshire	Yorkshire Water Authority	Blackburn Meadows, Sheffield	Side tipping wagons	Rail traffic ceased

This list is far from complete and the author would be extremely grateful for corrections and details of any additional locations, together with a description of the wagons operated. (Email - ops@irsociety.co.uk)

92

WAGON BUILDERS, REPAIRERS AND FINANCIERS
(Source : Rylands directory, 1947)

NAME	ADDRESS	PRINCIPAL CONSTRUCTION AND NOTES
Alfred Allen & Son Ltd	Gornal, near Dudley, Staffordshire	N.G. Tipping & quarry wagons, not railway specialists. Reg. 7/1907
W.G. Allen & Son (Tipton) Ltd	Princes End, Tipton, Staffordshire	Mostly N.G. hopper, tipping & quarry wagons. Reg. 6/1909
Sir William Arrol & Co	85 Dunn Street, Bridgeton, Glasgow	Transporters, transfer cars, scale cars, specialist plant & cranes. Reg. 6/1893
Ashmore, Benson, Pease & Co Ltd	Parkfield Works, Stockton on Tees. Also – Imperial Boiler Works, Stockton-on-Tees, and Bowesfield Foundry, Stockton-on-Tees	Transporters, makers of all steelworks & coke works plant; controlled by Power Gas Corporation Ltd
W.G. Bagnall Ltd	Castle Engine Works, Stafford	Tipping wagons. Reg. 7/1887
William Bain & Co Ltd	Lochrin Ironworks, Coatbridge, Lanarkshire	Tipping wagons, light railway equipment. Reg. 7/1908
E.E. Baguley Ltd	Burton-on-Trent, Staffordshire	Railway locomotives & wagons. Reg. /1932
Bartles (Carr Brea) Ltd	Carr Brea, Redruth, Cornwall	Quarry wagons, mining specialists. Reg. /1940
J.B. Beadman & Sons & Co Ltd	Lawkholme Wagon Works, Keighley, Yorkshire	Railway wagon builders & repairers. Reg. 12/1906
Bell & Son (Doncaster) Ltd	1 St. Sepulchre Gate, Doncaster, Yorkshire	Railway wagon contractors. Reg. /1939 & 'Wagons' Reg. /1944
John Bellamy Ltd	13 Byng Street, West Ferry Road, Millwall London. E14	Tank wagons shells only?
Birmingham Railway Carriage & Wagon Co Ltd	Smethwick, Staffordshire	Railway carriages & wagons, steel underframe specialist. Reg. 3/1855
Bolton Railway Wagon & Iron Works Co Ltd	33 Viking Street, Bolton, Lancashire	Works – Manchester Road, Bolton. Reg. 8/1896
British Wagon Co Ltd	23 Moorgate, Rotherham, Yorkshire	Owners & Financiers
Buchanan & Co (Wagons) Ltd	Easterhouse, Bailleston, Glasgow	Builders & repairers. Reg. 7/1935
Thomas Burnett & Co Ltd	Hexthorpe Wagon & Wheel Works, Doncaster, Yorkshire	Wagons & components. Reg. 12/1899
Butterley Co Ltd	Butterley Works, Butterley, Derbyshire	General engineers & steel and iron railway wagon builders, founded 1790. Reg. 4/1888

WAGON BUILDERS, REPAIRERS AND FINANCIERS

(Source : Rylands directory, 1947)

NAME	ADDRESS	PRINCIPAL CONSTRUCTION AND NOTES
Cambrian Wagon Works Ltd	Maindy, Cardiff, Glamorganshire	Railway wagon builders & repairers, incl. tipping wagons. Incorporating Welsh Wagon Works Ltd and Cambrian Wagon Co Ltd, re-registered 11/1935. Part of Powell Dyffryn Group
R.J. & M. Carr Ltd	LNER Hammerton Street, Bradford, Yorkshire	Railway wagons. Reg. 8/1923
Central Wagon Co Ltd	Causeway Avenue, Warrington, Lancashire	Wagon financiers
Central Wagon Co Ltd	Higher Ince, Wigan, Lancashire	Railway wagon builders & repairers, owns share capital of Moy's Wagon Co Ltd, Ince Waggon & Iron Works Co Ltd, Preston Wagon Co Ltd, Charles Godfrey Ltd and control of the Doncaster Wagon Co Ltd. Reg. 9/1911.
Chorley Wagons Ltd	Springs Branch, Wigan, Lancashire	Railway wagons & colliery tub builders
Cravens Railway Carriage & Wagon Co Ltd	Darnall, Sheffield, South Yorkshire	Wagon builders incl. tipping, tank & hopper wagons, specialist in steel underframes. Reg. 7/1891
Cutbill, King & Co Ltd	London	Machinery merchants, incl. tank wagons. Reg. 11/1921
W.H. Davis & Sons	Langwith, Mansfield, Derbyshire	Railway wagon & wheel manufacturers. Reg. 5/1908
Derbyshire Carriage & Wagon Co Ltd	New Whittington, Chesterfield, Derbyshire	Railway wagon builders & repairers. Reg. 11/1913
Dewhurst	Sheffield	Ladles & transfer cars
Doncaster Wagon Co Ltd	Danum Works, Doncaster, Yorkshire;.	And Ince, Wigan, Lancashire; Northfield Works, Rotherham and Clay Cross, Chesterfield. Controlled by Central Wagon Co Ltd. Reg. 6/1931,
Edward Eastwood	Railway Wagon Works, Brimington Road, Chesterfield, Derbyshire	Wagon builder & repairer
Fairfield Shipbuilding & Engineering Co Ltd	Chepstow, Monmouthshire & Fairfield Works, Govan, Glasgow	Shipbuilders, steel fabricators & railway wagon builders. Reg. 7/1889
Firth Bros Ltd	Dearne Works, Scissett, Huddersfield, Yorkshire	Tipping & hopper wagon, specialist in colliery tubs. Reg. 7/1927

94

WAGON BUILDERS, REPAIRERS AND FINANCIERS
(Source : Rylands directory, 1947)

NAME	ADDRESS	PRINCIPAL CONSTRUCTION AND NOTES
Frazers & Chalmers Engineering Works	Fraser Road, Erith, Kent	Conveying & transporting plant. Proprietors – The General Electric Co Ltd
Robert Frazer & Sons Ltd	Hebburn on Tyne, Co.Durham	Wagon repairers and general iron & steel merchants
Arthur Gibson & Son Ltd	Priory Sidings, Hessle, Hull, Yorkshire	Railway wagon builders and repairers, depots at Gascoigne Wood, Milford & New Clee, Grimsby
William Gittus & Son Ltd	Barnsley Junction Wagon & Wheel Works, Penistone, Sheffield, Yorkshire	Wagon builder and repairer. Reg. 6/1918
Glamorgan Wagon Co Ltd	Cliffside, Forest Road, Penarth, Glamorganshire	Wagon hirers & financiers. Reg. 11/1913
A. Gloster	Imperial House, Dominion Street, London. EC2	Agent for USA light railway equipment including Sisal wagons
Gloucester Railway Carriage & Wagon Co Ltd	Bristol Road, Gloucester	Railway wagon builder, tank wagons, specialised in steel underframes. Reg. 9/1889; interests in Wagon Repairs Ltd
Charles Godfrey Ltd	Peterborough, Northamptonshire	Railway wagon repairers. Reg. 10/1938
M. & W. Grazebrook	Netherton Ironworks, Dudley, Worcestershire	Tank wagons
Hadfields Ltd	East Hecla Works, Sheffield, Yorkshire	Tipping wagons, wheels, axles & forgings.
D. G. Hall & Co Ltd	Coverack Road, Newport, Monmouthshire	Railway wagon builders & repairers
Head, Wrightson & Co Ltd	Thornaby on Tees, Stockton on Tees, Yorkshire	General heavy engineers & steel founders, hoppers, tipping, tank & quarry wagons, and transporters
Robert Hudson Ltd	Railtrux House, Meadow Lane, Leeds,	Light railway equipment manufacturers, tipping & hopper wagons. Reg. 4/1914
Thomas Hunter Ltd	Rugby, Warwickshire	Railway wagon builders & repairers. Reg. 10/1922
Hurst Nelson & Co Ltd	The Glasgow Rolling Stock and Plant Works, Motherwell, Lanarkshire	Railway Wagon builders,. tank wagons, specialists in steel underframes. Reg. 2/1909
Ince Wagon & Ironworks Co Ltd	Lower Ince, Wigan, Lancashire	Railway wagon builders; capital held by Central Wagon Co Ltd

WAGON BUILDERS, REPAIRERS AND FINANCIERS

(Source : Rylands directory, 1947)

NAME	ADDRESS	PRINCIPAL CONSTRUCTION AND NOTES
John Ingham & Sons Ltd	Wakefield Road, Ossett, and Middlestown, Wakefield, Yorkshire	Tipping wagons & colliery tub manufacturer
E.C. & J. Keay Ltd	Runnymeade, Henley in Arden, near Birmingham	General engineering quarry wagons
J. Kenworthy & Son Ltd	Fartown, Lockwood, Huddersfield, Yorkshire	Railway wagon builders and repairers. Reg. 7/1925
Lancashire & Yorkshire Waggon Co Ltd	Wagon Works, Green Lane, Heywood, Lancashire	Railway wagon builders
Little & Angus	Ironworks Road, Barrow in Furness Lancashire	Railway wagon builders
T. Locker & Co	Old Whittington, Chesterfield Derbyshire	Railway wagon builders
J. & H. Lowe (Cranes) Ltd	Oldham, Lancashire	Transporters
P. & W. MacLellan Ltd	129 Trongate, Glasgow	Tank wagons
Marcroft Wagons Ltd	Gloucester House, Swansea, Glamorganshire	
Marple & Gillott Ltd	Sheffield, Yorkshire (also Gateshead & London)	Tipping wagons
M.E. Engineering Ltd	London	Tipping wagons
Metropolitan-Cammell Carriage and Wagon Co Ltd	Saltley, Birmingham	Specialist in steel underframes, tank wagons
Midland Railway Carriage and Wagon Co Ltd	Saltley, Birmingham.	Tipping & tank wagons
Mitchell Engineering Co Ltd	Peterborough	Transporters
Motherwell Wagon & Rolling Stock Co Ltd	Flemington, Motherwell, Lanarkshire	
W.G. Moreton & Co Ltd	Masborough Works, Rotherham, Yorkshire	Builder & repairer
Moys Wagon Co Ltd	Peterborough, Northamptonshire	
North Central Wagon & Finance Co Ltd	Moorgate, Rotherham, Yorkshire	
Northern Waggon Co Ltd	Causeway Avenue, Warrington, Lancashire	
North Glamorgan Wagon Co Ltd	Cliffside, Forest Road, Penarth, Glamorganshire	Wagon financiers
North Wales Wagon Co Ltd	Queensferry, Chester	

WAGON BUILDERS, REPAIRERS AND FINANCIERS
(Source : Rylands directory, 1947)

NAME	ADDRESS	PRINCIPAL CONSTRUCTION AND NOTES
R.Y. Pickering & Co Ltd	Wishaw. Lanarkshire	Hopper & tank wagons, specialist in steel underframes
Preston Wagon Co Ltd	Marsh Lane, Preston, Lancashire	
Pressed Steel Co Ltd	Linwood, Paisley, Scotland	
Principality Wagon Co Ltd	Ferry Road, Grangetown, Cardiff, Glamorganshire	Builders & repairers
Railway & General Products Co Ltd	London	
Railway Mine & Plantation Equipment Ltd	London	
Renishaw Park Wagon and Sawmills Ltd	169 Norfolk Street, Sheffield	
Wm. Rigley & Sons Ltd	Bulwell Forest, Nottingham.	Hopper, tank & quarry wagons, pit tubs, building, leasing and repairs,
Railway Mine & Plantation Equipment Ltd	London	Hopper wagons
Chas. Roberts & Co Ltd	Horbury Junction, Wakefield, Yorkshire	Tank, tipping & quarry wagons, specialists in steel underframes
Rolling Stock Co Ltd	Albert Hill, Darlington, Co.Durham	Repairers
J. Sharland & Sons Ltd	Stairfoot, Barnsley, Yorkshire	
Sheepbridge Coal and Iron Co Ltd	Sheepbridge, Chesterfield, Derbyshire	Tipping wagons
South Staffordshire Wagon Co	Blowers Green Wagon Works, Dudley, Worcestershire	
Standard Steel Co (1929) Ltd	Croydon	Tipping wagons
Stothert & Pitt Ltd	Bath	Transporters
Strachan & Henshaw Ltd	Bristol	Transporters
Taff Wagon Co Ltd	Ferry Road, Grangetown, Cardiff, Glamorganshire	
Tees Side Bridge & Engineering Works Ltd	Middlesbrough	Tank wagons, specialists in steel underframes
Francis Theakston (1933) Ltd	Weybridge	Tipping wagons
Tondu Engineering & Wagon Co Ltd	Tondu, Glamorganshire	
G.R. Turner Ltd	Langley Mill. Nottinghamshire	Tank & quarry wagons
Thos W. Ward Ltd	Sheffield, Yorkshire	Tank wagons
S. Rhodes & Co Ltd	Sheffield, Birmingham & Liverpool	Hopper & quarry wagons

WAGON BUILDERS, REPAIRERS AND FINANCIERS
(Source : Rylands directory, 1947)

NAME	ADDRESS	PRINCIPAL CONSTRUCTION AND NOTES
Wagon Finance Corporation Ltd	64 Fargate, Sheffield, Yorkshire	Wagon financiers
Wagon Repairs Ltd	41a John Bright Street, Birmingham	Repairers
Wantage Engineering Co Ltd	Wantage	Tipping wagons
Watts, Hardy & Co Ltd	Howden, Willington Quay, Northumberland	
The Wellman, Smith & Owen Engineering Corporation Ltd	Victoria Street, London	Transporters
West of England Wagon Co	Lydney, Gloucestershire	Repairer
R. White & Sons. (Engineers) Ltd	Widnes. Lancashire	Transporters & tipping wagons
Hy. Williams Ltd	Hebburn, Co.Durham	
Wigan Wagon Co	Ince, Wigan, Lancashire	
F.T. Wright Ltd	Arnold Road, Nottingham, Nottinghamshire	

INDEX OF ROLLING STOCK DESCRIBED

INDEX OF ROLLING STOCK DESCRIBED

* indicates that a drawing accompanies this entry